CRIES FOR HELP

Women Without a Voice

Women's Prisons in the 1970s

Myra Hindley and Her Contemporaries

Joanna Kozubska

 WATERSIDE PRESS

Cries for Help
Women Without a Voice
Women's Prisons in the 1970s
Myra Hindley and Her Contemporaries

ISBN 978-1-909976-05-4 (Paperback)
ISBN 978-1-908162-69-4 (Epub ebook)
ISBN 978-1-908162-70-0 (Adobe ebook)

Cover design © 2014 Waterside Press. Front cover drawing by Graham Savage. Design by www.gibgob.com.

Main UK distributor Gardners Books, 1 Whittle Drive, Eastbourne, East Sussex, BN23 6QH. Tel: +44 (0)1323 521777; sales@gardners.com; www.gardners.com

North American distribution Ingram Book Company, One Ingram Blvd, La Vergne, TN 37086, USA. Tel: (+1) 615 793 5000; inquiry@ingramcontent.com

Cataloguing-In-Publication Data A catalogue record for this book can be obtained from the British Library.

Printed by CPI Group, Chippenham, UK.

e-book *Cries for Help* is available as an ebook and also to subscribers of Myilibrary, Dawsonera, ebrary, and Ebscohost.

Published 2014 by
Waterside Press
Sherfield Gables
Sherfield-on-Loddon
Hook, Hampshire
United Kingdom RG27 0JG

Telephone +44(0)1256 882250
E-mail enquiries@watersidepress.co.uk
Online catalogue WatersidePress.co.uk

Contents

About the Author

Joanna Kozubska is Professor of Managerial Communications at the International Management Centres and its Vice President, UK.

After teaching in the UK and then Africa with Voluntary Service Overseas, she worked as an assistant governor at Holloway Prison and other HM Prison Service establishments (1970-1977) then as Head of the Special Unit for Disturbed and Disordered Young People at Aycliffe School, County Durham.

During her prison career, she hit the news in the 1970s after borstal girls climbed onto the roof of Holloway demanding that she should not be transferred from their wing (*Chapter 10*). As explained in *Chapter 5*, she later escaped notice after Myra Hindley, the Moors Murderer, was escorted out of the gates of Holloway for a headline-making 'walk in the park'.

Joanna Kozubska holds an MBA and DPhil. She published her first book *The Seven Keys of Charisma* in 1997, writes on related topics and is a well-known exponent of Action Learning. In 2012 she became an altruistic kidney donor. She is Chair of the Friends of Guys Marsh.

Architectural Drawings

The drawings in this book are by Graham Savage based on historical photographs and materials. He has been an Associate of the Royal Institute of British Architects since 1967 and his artwork developed from illustrating both his own projects and commissions from other architectural practices. He is a member of the Society of Architectural Illustrators and also the Society of Graphic Fine Art.

Acknowledgements

This book has been four years in the writing.

Ruth Eade and Bob Mackenzie convinced me I had a story worth telling. My friends from the Writers' Cottage in Anglesey cheered me on. Ann Booth ensured I put myself into the book. John Taylor saw so much more in what I gave him to read. Angela Niemeyer Eastwood and Andrea Hessay gave me a necessary objective view. Mags Burgin, Jen Stack, Clare Denby, Angela Knight, Terry Tucker and Lara Harris read chapters and cheered me on. Val Lowman encouraged me with her passion and enthusiasm. Patrick and Katie Brown gave me their wise counsel, their time and interest over the long period of writing and asked after the book every time we met.

In dark days, novelist Mario Reading got me started again.

My Prison Service colleagues were magnificent in their support: Colin Honey confirmed in my mind what I wanted to write. Ann Hair couldn't have been more helpful, jogging my memory, reminding me of how things had been, and researching information we had both forgotten. David Faulkner encouraged me, gave me his time and advice, read and commented on my work. Muriel Allen and Audrey Stern gave me their support and their stories. Monica Carden and Judy Gibbons shared their memories. Pat Bartholomew read chapters and gave me enthusiastic feedback.

Phil Wheatley cleared the way for me to use the letters in the book and gave me encouraging feedback when he later read the manuscript.

The Hon. Mary Morrison and Min Wood supported me in so many ways.

My school friends were a huge support. Judith Kelley, Gaynor McCarthy, Sue Di Girolamo and Marion Put Picton were interested and fascinated. Mary Simpson took a draft to bed with her and read it after a tough days' work and reported a real fascination. Sue Jones read the final draft and gave me much valued and wonderful feedback. My family, Shena, Danuta and Gerald offered continuous support.

Graham Savage contributed the fantastic drawings.

Rosemary Macdonald gave me reassuring final feedback.

Mandy Little, my agent, encouraged me and kept me writing.

My new colleagues in the Friends of Guys Marsh gave me unbiased encouragement.

Bryan Gibson, Waterside Press, believed in the project and said 'yes'. Alex steered the illustrations into the book with much care.

Most importantly, I am indebted to all the women who wrote letters to me and who gave me permission to use their material.

Jo Denby took my photograph and but for Jo I would not have started or completed. She read each draft and has been my support, encouragement and editor throughout.

Thank you.

Joanna Kozubska

February 2014

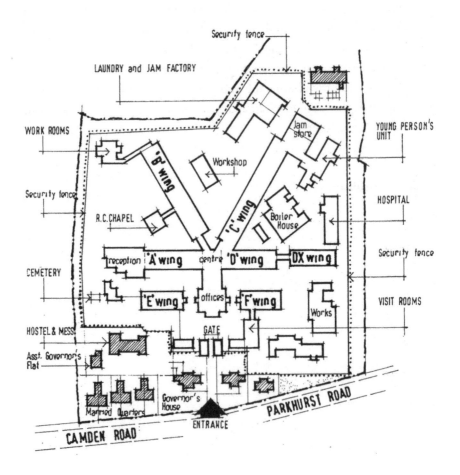

Site plan of the original old Holloway Prison taken
from historical drawings made in the 1850s.
There had been a number of changes and alterations by
1971 but the structure was essentially the same.

List of illustrations

For all those who wrote letters to me

For all the women whose lives I shared for a short time

Thank you.

For Jo

With love

Foreword: Lord David Ramsbotham

Like Joanna Kozubska much of my thinking about the imprisonment of women is based on what I saw of their treatment and conditions in HMP Holloway, the largest women's prison in Great Britain. In her case that included practical experience, over a number of years, in different staff posts. In mine it began with my first ever prison inspection as HM Chief Inspector of Prisons in 1995, in only my second week in office. I was intrigued that she should have chosen the subtitle 'Women Without a Voice — Prisons in the 1970s', because the fact that women did not seem to have a voice within the Prison Service hierarchy was one of my main concerns after abandoning my inspection. Throughout my career in another operational service, the Army, I had been used to a chain of command in which someone, some named person, was responsible and accountable for every function or activity, at every level. Naïvely I thought that that was normal, as it was true of the business in which I worked for two years, in the hospital that I chaired and the school of which I was a governor. Uniquely however it remains not so of the Prison Service, as I found when I asked the acting Director General — the Director General had just been sacked — if I could see the Director of Women, to be told that such a post did not exist, nor was any member of the Prisons Board responsible or accountable for women, policy being the responsibility of a civil servant in the policy department.

I walked out of that inspection because I was so appalled that any country, let alone my own, could treat vulnerable women in the way that I saw in Holloway in 1995, and particularly that neither Ministers or the Prison Service appeared to have taken any action to rectify faults that had been pointed-out to them for months by the independent Board of Visitors. As with an Army unit, found, on inspection, not to be fit for its operational purpose, I gave the authorities a list of points that I expected to be corrected before I returned, unannounced, to re-inspect in six months.

Four of these have echoes in Joanna Kozubska's book, because they illustrate points that she makes. Injuries to women being recorded on diagrams
of men's bodies, because the Prison Service did not issue any diagrams of
females. Hearing the dull thuds of women banging their heads against the
walls of their cells in the large and allegedly specialist Mental Health Unit,
but finding no psychiatrist or psychiatric nurses on duty. Being asked by a
young mother whether it was right that she had been in chains while giving
birth, and, on questioning the female Governor, being told that 'It was
regulations'. Finding two 15-year-old girls in the ante-natal unit, put there
not because they were pregnant—which they were not—but because, in
the words of the midwife, 'They did not know where else to put them'. She
then added 'I'm an Ibo, from Nigeria, which is meant to be less civilised
than here, but I have to tell you that I have seen nothing so inhuman and
disgusting as the way they treat women in Holloway'.

During that never-to-be-forgotten week, I learned three generalities
that continue to be true today. Firstly, since 1962, when the prison system
was brought under Home Office control, on the abolition of the Prison
Commission, the cult of managerialism has taken over from operational
leadership. This was marked by the abolition of the Women's Prison Service
and the separate Women's Department, leading to impersonal management
by civil service diktat, targets and performance indicators. I very much doubt
if I would have found what I did in Holloway had any of the giants of the
Women's Service, who so clearly inspired the author, been in post.

Secondly, everything in a prison depends on good staff/prisoner relationships. Unless things are right for staff, nothing will be right for prisoners.
Many prison governors under the Prison Commission were ex-members
of the Armed Forces, appointed to lead the staff, not to oversee prisoners,
which was left to the professionals. Staff leadership, and directed leadership of Governors, are now absent, with the result that staff feel leaderless,
particularly when it comes to developing the all-important relationships with
prisoners. Members of staff, who show an interest in them, possibly for the
first time in their lives, can be key factors in persuading someone to change
their life around, from law-breaker to law-abider, and must be encouraged to
do so. Without a Director to fight for career development or training, staff
in women's prisons will always be the poor relation of their more numerous

colleagues in male prisons, to the disadvantage of women prisoners.

Thirdly, prisoners can be broadly categorised into 'the sad, the mad and the bad'. Of these the incorrigibly bad are by far the smallest number. Joanna Kozubska illustrates this with numerous examples of sad and mad people, for whom prison today, with its focus on punishment, is the wrong place. In describing her attempts to help some of the women she was responsible for, both young and old, to turn their lives around, she illustrates, all too vividly, the desperate conditions from which they came, and to which they would return, and the frustrations experienced by inadequately resourced staff, in trying to help them.

Her story may have echoes of the 1970s, but, sadly, it rings all too true today. Whatever else they are, prisoners and staff are fellow human beings, whom the authorities must recognise as such. Therefore I hope that those authorities in particular will read and reflect on her brutally honest, human and very relevant book.

Lord Ramsbotham

HM Chief Inspector of Prisons for England and Wales 1995–2001

The Centre—The hub of the prison with its steel key safe and polished table
(see page 34)

Introduction: A Journey through Letters

When people ask me why I joined the Prison Service most expect me to say I wanted to 'help' people. Nothing was further from the truth. I had no explicitly altruistic motives. The salary was much better than I could expect as a teacher and—on reflection—I suspect I rather fancied being called 'Mam'!

I look back on my years in the service with affection and gratitude. I enjoyed myself enormously and I learned so much about myself and others. I made good friends amongst staff and inmates and enjoy many of these relationships today. This period of my life made more impact on me than any other. It left more scars than anything since but it also gave me some of my most vivid and formative experiences. My purpose in writing this book is to reflect both mine and inmates' views of the women's service in the 1970s and to give the inmates who wrote to me a voice over 35 years on. I want to give them an opportunity to put their side of the story, albeit mediated at times by my own personal perspective.

We were all Myra Hindley's contemporaries.

Initially, I served as an assistant governor II—as the rank was called in those days—at Her Majesty's Prison Holloway. I was in charge of the Borstal Recall Wing and then D Wing for long termers and lifers. This was followed by a posting to HM Borstal, Hindley in Lancashire. A year later, in 1974, I was promoted to assistant governor I and took up my new post as deputy governor at HM Borstal Bullwood Hall.

All my postings were memorable—I enjoyed my relationships with the prison staff and inmates. As an assistant governor II, I was responsible for the security, care and training of inmates on my wing or house. I believed that a major part of my role was to create and ensure the best quality of life possible for those in my charge—both inmates and staff. As far as the inmates were concerned, this meant creating environments in which they would feel able to take advantage of the treatment and training opportunities available. I saw prison as a time for people to take stock and make decisions about their future and change their behaviour patterns—if that was what was required. It never occurred to me that their crimes should influence the way I saw them or treated them. My relationships were based on my view of people and of course, the way they responded to me. I hope I treated people with respect and I expected them to reciprocate. Looking back I see a naïve and idealistic young woman in her 20s—who probably personified the saying 'Fools rush in where angels fear to tread'. I walked a fine line between over-involvement and lack of objectivity—and professional care and concern for the individual.

Following each of my postings many of those in my care wrote to me for some time afterwards. I have no idea why, but I kept all their letters; I have a unique collection of original material—some hundred or so letters, poems, cards and artefacts. These I have read and re-read in the context of my own memories.

Many of these letters are from ordinary women, ordinary boys, ordinary mums and dads and friends. Some are from notorious prisoners. Some are from deeply disturbed individuals. They contain comments about life in prison, thoughts about events, writers' feelings about themselves and their families, views on staff and on the prison system. The letters reflect the relationships I enjoyed with the writers.

Whilst at Holloway, I encouraged the girls on the Borstal Recall Wing and the women on D Wing to use their creative talents to write for and produce magazines. Some of the writing in these publications is poignant and quite revealing and I have included extracts where I feel that they add an important perspective.

Amalgamated with the men's Prison Service in the mid-1970s, the Women's Prison Service no longer exists as a separate entity. The world of the 1970s no longer exists. Both belong to a seemingly gentler time—before the drug culture and fear of terrorism had taken a hold on prisons and society, infecting people and their environments.

The letters themselves are frozen in time. The writers' views and comments are their own, written from their particular perspective. They reflect the truth of their situation as they saw it. I have used the letters in two ways—reciting comments to illustrate points I want to make and, most importantly, looking at the significance of the writer's words.

I have not corrected the spelling, grammar or punctuation in the letters.

They are reproduced in the book as they were written.

I have included letters from prison officers and senior management because their thoughts and views are as important as those of the women they looked after. Staff played a significant part in creating the environment and I hope that their words will help to illustrate the atmosphere in which we all lived. We were all ordinary mortals living in an extraordinary environment.

I have included letters from parents and friends and looking back, I feel privileged to have earned their trust. Those left outside the gates very often have a much harder time than those who serve sentences.

My memories and the comments I make are with the benefit of hindsight and seen through spectacles tinted with a little scholarship, much experience and maturity. I am presenting my truth as I see it now and it is difficult to know how different my views are from those I held at the time. I have written from memory — often prompted by the letters themselves and I realise that colleagues who shared my experiences at the time may well have different memories and interpretations, and they may be coming from different perspectives.

The copyright of the letters in my possession remains with the authors. I have used extracts of letters in the main. Apart from one or two instances I have changed names, précised and paraphrased, particularly where words would betray an identity. It is not my intention to identify, upset or offend anyone. I have frequently described individuals who in reality are composites of one or two real people to disguise identities.

I thought long and hard about Myra Hindley. Should I include her or leave her out? Would her reputation detract from what I wanted to say — would including her be detrimental to this book? She was a major part of my life at Holloway and leaving her out would mean that I was not being entirely honest about my experience. Her letters to me illustrate another side to her. I will be damned if I do and damned if I don't. I decided to include her.

I fully realise that the picture of women in prison that I have painted here is not one most people would recognise. But it is my most vivid picture; I did experience some violence, uncouthness, manipulation and cruelty but this was not my overriding experience. That kind of behaviour provided a pale backdrop against which women lived out their sentences, often positively.

I realise that some people will find my views offensive particularly where

I have expressed positive feelings about people who were convicted criminals. I make no apologies. As I express later in the book, I met these women after they had committed their offence; my relationship with them was not influenced by first-hand experience of their crimes—on the whole, I didn't see them at their worst or most troubled. I met them living their everyday lives in prison.

Revisiting the past—looking at my youthful self has been enormously enjoyable, also painful. I have written about myself to help the reader understand where I was coming from and to provide some kind of picture of the receiver of the letters.

I have deliberately not written chronologically. I have taken liberties with my readers expecting them to follow me as I jump around in what might appear to be a haphazard fashion. I hope you will bear with me as one thought leads to another and as I strive to keep your interest.

I have included five cameo pieces—unrelated to any letters—which have enabled me to tell you more about the women I worked with and the job that I did.

Reading the letters, remembering all the women who wrote them, and one or two borstal boys—has been a pleasure. I do worry that I did not reply to some of these letters and hope that I have been forgiven. I know that many of these women will no longer be with us. Some I know are dead, others I imagine will be. I know that some are living useful, fulfilled lives. One or two will have had a hard passage. All of them left something with me and I remember them with affection. I hope that at least one or two of them might read this book and remember the good moments in what was probably a dark period of their lives.

I am grateful to my Prison Service colleagues for their care, friendship, help and support when we worked together and as I wrote.

'Miss K'

Joanna Kozubska

February 2014

Cameo 1: A glimpse of a murderer

Just a few hours before, the small middle-aged woman sitting in front of me had killed her husband with a kitchen knife. She sat in a daze seemingly uncomprehending of her situation and yet apparently aware that she had changed her world for ever. She was devastated and shocked.

In 1971, I was spending a couple of days at Risley Remand Centre whilst doing my initial training at Wakefield Staff College and was sitting with the reception officers. They were admitting a woman straight from a magistrates' court where she had been remanded in custody. The long process leading up to custody and a criminal trial starts at a magistrates' court but by the time offenders get to a prison remand centre they may have been in police cells for days waiting to be charged. This was different. Margaret had stabbed her husband just hours before and had been taken to court almost immediately. I had never met anyone who had committed such a serious crime so shortly after the event. Prison staff are not police officers. They do not see what offenders have done and they do not have to clear up the mess and manage the aftermath. They deal with the individual in a different context — one which is far removed from the event itself.

The woman appeared to be in deep shock. Looking at her, no one would have ever imagined that she had committed the most serious of crimes less than 24 hours ago.

The officers dealt kindly with Margaret. The police had brought a bag of her clothes with her; she was given a bath, a change of clothes and put in a cell on her own. I doubt Margaret had ever had to undress in front of strangers or to have a bath under the gaze of watchful staff, however kindly. When she was settled into her cell I went to see her again. The wing was noisy with the shouting, laughing and yelling brash young women and old hands who knew the ropes — all making the best of things — sharing cigarettes and talking. Margaret was the odd one out that evening.

There wasn't much I could say — I could only just *be there* with her. I do remember asking her if there was anyone she needed to contact — did she need letter writing materials? There were no telephone calls home in those days although I could have made a call for her. But no — she was too ashamed to write to anyone. Margaret was

42, middle-class and well to do. Prison would have been the ultimate disgrace for someone of her background and yet here she was. The police said that they thought she had been driven to it but Margaret appeared to be battling with what she had done and had certainly started her punishment. She had lost all her privacy and control of her world. She was in a place which, in the past, would have been unthinkable for her. And she had murdered her husband.

I met Margaret about a year later at Askham Grange open prison. She was sharing a room with about four other women and appeared settled and indeed reasonably happy. She had been given a relatively short sentence and, as she was no threat to anyone, had been sent to an open prison quite quickly. The staff were pleased with the way Margaret had settled into the routine. She had adapted and developed a set of coping skills; she knuckled down to do her sentence with as little hassle as possible. I talked to her briefly but her memory of the dreadful day we met was blurred and I doubt she really remembered me. She was keen to get off to do good works in the village with her roommates! I didn't see Margaret again but the impact she made on me influenced the way I saw imprisonment and my understanding of domestic crime.

Margaret gave me a little insight into the trauma that many prisoners experience prior to their coming into prison and the immediate effect that violent crime can have on the perpetrator herself. I witnessed someone existing in a world of guilt and imprisonment totally outside her previous experience but who within a few short months had worked out how she could manage in her new surroundings. I suspect her sense of punishment would have changed over her time. The first few days at Risley would have been like Hell for Margaret — locked up to *be* punished. By the time she got to Askham Grange I suspect she would have seen being away from her home *as* punishment. And yet Margaret would be the first person to say that she needed to be punished for what she had done.

CHAPTER I

Joining the Service

My father, who was Polish, had been captured by the Germans, escaped, was interned in Switzerland during the Second World War; he eventually escaped to England via France and Spain, arriving here in 1942. Some 20 years later he was imprisoned in Austria on suspicion of smuggling aircraft parts. My mother found the bail money and he came back home. This was the sum total of my knowledge and experience of prison when I applied to join the service in 1970.

The hot dust and excitement of my Voluntary Service Overseas (VSO) posting in Africa seemed a long time ago as I sat in the train returning home from London in 1970. Wondering what to do next, I scanned the paper for inspiration. My eye alighted on an advert asking me if I wanted to do 'social work with management' which seemed an attractive proposition. The advert was for an assistant governor post within Her Majesty's Prison Service.

I had trained as a teacher and enjoyed my two years in Africa immensely but knew I didn't want to teach. I think I was good in the classroom but I was also pretty bad at marking—spelling not being a strong suit. Preparation was a chore. I was also sure it would be years before I was given any kind of real responsibility even for the stationery cupboard. I set about looking for an alternative career and found the Prison Service.

As a prospective assistant governor, I would be a civil servant which meant that I had to go through the appropriate civil service selection process. I passed the preliminary sift and was invited for interview in London. There were three people on the panel. I only remember one of them, Mrs Joanna Kelley who was the assistant director in charge of the women's prison service. I enjoyed the interview and as I didn't really have anything to lose I remember being relaxed. All went well. A letter soon followed:

Home Office

London

6 May 1970

Madam

I am directed by the Secretary of State to inform you that you have been appointed as an Assistant governor, Class II, in the Prison Service, and a Certificate of Qualification dated 23 April 1970 has been issued in your favour by the Civil Service Commissioners.

You will be required to join the Prison Service at the Staff College, Love Lane, Wakefield, on Monday 28th September 1970 to undergo a training course.

The three page tightly written letter goes on to include the terms and conditions of my employment.

I spent seven years at Talbot Heath School, Bournemouth where I was a boarder. I loved school. My mother kept all my reports and I can see myself through the eyes of my housemistress and teachers. I worked hard—sometimes with little to show for it in terms of results but I always tried. Not a term went by but I was head of dormitory, the common room or a form leader and latterly head of hall and school prefect.

I went straight from school to Hereford College of Education—gap years hadn't been invented. I joined everything and did everything. I was elected onto the student council in my second year and in my third I was elected president of the student union.

I learned much. Hereford was so different from Talbot Heath. Students came from all walks of life. They had differing experiences and expectations; some spoke differently—we had a range of regional accents—Welsh and Scottish, Brummy and Scouse. I have one particularly clear memory from my Hereford days. Sitting on the top deck of a bus, I remember having a long discussion about the results of the trial of the moors murderers. As trainee teachers we were focused on children; we were horrified with what we had read in the newspaper on the evening of May 6th 1966. It was beyond our comprehension that a young woman, just four years older than we were, from the same part of Manchester as some of our friends, could possibly have committed such appalling crimes. We found it shocking and unbelievable.

What was I to do after my three years at Hereford? If I was going to have to teach, I decided that I didn't want to teach in the UK. At the end of my college course I decided to see what VSO might offer me; I applied to be a volunteer and was accepted.

At 21, in September 1967, greatly excited, I set off for Tanzania but, if I am honest, with just a little trepidation. After various adventures, I found myself teaching English, Geography and Religious Knowledge or Dini as it was called, at Tabora Girls School, Tanzania.

Several hundred girls attended the school from all over the country. Tabora was the number one girls' boarding school in the country. All the students were Tanzanian although the staff was predominantly European. I fitted into the school easily—after all, I knew about boarding schools and Tabora was modelled on the British system.

Looking back at myself in my mid-20s, over 40 years ago now, I joined the prison service knowing about institutions. I could 'do' institutions. I had lived in three single sex institutions for 14 years—over half my life. They held no fears for me. Institutions were positive places—places where people cared for others and were cared for. I joined the prison service with bags of leadership experience but with some awareness of my own frailty as a leader, as well as real confidence in my own ability. I had lived in different cultures, I could cope with and enjoyed difference; I knew I was resourceful and could push boundaries successfully.

I had several months to wait before going to the Prison Service Staff College, Wakefield, to begin my training. The interviewing panel had suggested that, if my application was successful, I might like to become a temporary prison officer and gain experience 'on the landings' before going to Wakefield. This would provide me with valuable knowledge about the realities of prison life. I agreed with alacrity and in the summer of 1970 found myself at the gates of HM Borstal Bullwood Hall, the only closed borstal for girls in the country. I had no idea what to expect.

H M Borstal
Bullwood Hall
Miss J Kozijbska
Dorset

20 May 1970

Dear Miss Kozijbska

Thank you for your letter, which came to me as the Governor, Miss Parry, is away at the moment.

We shall be pleased to have you here as a Temporary Officer from August 1 until 12 September. I think it a long enough period for you to pick up some useful experience.

A room in the Officer's hostel would be available to you, if you wished to live in. otherwise it would mean your finding your own accommodation in the district. We have no mess at Bullwood, but cooking facilities, including utensils, are available in the hostel.

You will be paid at the temporary officer's rate of £19.0.6 per week less £2.1.3 per week for lodging, if you live in the hostel. As you say, you should bring your National Insurance card with you, also a P45 income tax form.

We would expect you to arrive during the morning of 1 August but perhaps you would confirm that nearer the time.

Please do not hesitate to telephone or write, if there is anything further you wish to know.

Your sincerely
J Kinsley
Dep Governor i/c

Ps Hours of duty including alternating weekends on and approximately 2 evening duties per week. JK

I made my way over to Hockley in Essex, not far from Southend, and finally drove down the tree lined approach to the borstal. Bullwood Hall was a purpose built institution — opened in 1962 in the grounds of an old Edwardian mansion called Bullwood Hall. The park was lovely with magnificent trees and the remains of formal gardens. The borstal itself was surrounded by a high netting fence topped with fierce barbed wire. Inside the fence, the building was sprawly; red brick and flat roofed, little white windows with geometrically patterned bars, arranged in long rows, two layers of them. Huge barred steel gates guarded the entrance.

Bullwood Hall was divided into three main houses — House One, Two and Three — each on two levels. In many ways these houses looked like modern interpretations of the old Victorian prison wings — cells on landings round two sides with space in the middle. On the upper floors the void was filled by wire netting which I later learned was to prevent inmates throwing themselves, or others, over the railings on to 'the flat', the floor below. Bullwood had two floors only, rather than the normal four of the old Victorian institutions. Two pairs of double doors guarded the single entrance to each house. Cells were single and double occupancy giving each house capacity for around 30 borstal girls with an assistant governor and team of officers to look after them. In total, Bullwood locked up a maximum of 97 girls every night.

I remember the houses themselves as Spartan and noisy. Low ceilings, no soft furnishings — hard metal chairs with wooden seats and similar tables, the odd newspaper or magazine and the occasional book; borstal girls shouting, music blaring and confident plainclothes officers getting on with the business of the day. I had heard all about 'slopping-out' and I assumed that the houses would smell. They didn't. No one — inmates or officers — wanted to live and work in smelly conditions so cleaning was well supervised and on the whole, well done.

I was to be a temporary officer for the summer. I was apprehensive but equally I remember being excited at the prospect of working in these tough surroundings. I probably had some kind of induction or look round the institution but I was there to work as an officer; I was put on the duty rota for House Two.

I enjoyed my time on 'the landings' and learned a great deal. Most of the officers were excellent role models for me. One or two were not and that in itself was a useful experience. I started to understand the nature of the relationships between the borstal girls and their officers. The girls were outwardly toughies, working hard and often successfully to cover up vulnerable personalities. Many had tragic stories to tell. The officers were outwardly strict and firm but always ready to show care and concern for their charges, whenever appropriate. Most of the officers went the extra mile for the girls. I began to understand the two edged sword of institutions. Many of the girls received more care and affection when serving their borstal sentences than they experienced outside with their own families and communities. No wonder many returned time after time. It was better inside.

Girls were released from borstal 'on licence'. This meant that they could be returned to borstal if they breached the terms of their licences — i.e. if they didn't do what they were told. The 'terms' stipulated where they had to live and what they could and couldn't do. There was an exhortation 'to live a good and useful life'. If they didn't comply — back they came — but to Holloway Borstal Recall — where I met some of them later.

I joined the 23rd Prison Service Staff Course in September 1970. We were 51 men and three women.

The Staff College itself — once the Imperial Staff College because it also trained overseas staff — was not dissimilar from a military officers' mess with the usual offices; public rooms of library, dining room, sitting rooms and classrooms. Accommodation was basic.

My colleagues came from a variety of backgrounds. Some had been prison officers, others came directly from the services and some, like me, from other professions such as social work and teaching. Our ages ranged from the mid-20s to 40 plus. I was at the younger end at 25.

The staff course was designed to prepare newly appointed assistant governors for their future roles. Assistant governors were the lowest form of 'commissioned officer' in military terms; not to be confused with the prison officers who had their own seniority structure as non-commissioned officers — again similar to the military. We studied basic psychology, sociology and criminology and, of course, we learned about the prison service itself. I think we did some basic management stuff too. But the real learning would come on the job — as I would find out.

Towards the end of the eight months the big day arrived. We were all given little brown envelopes enclosing letters hand written on that rather brittle white government paper. These told us to which establishments we would be posted as fully-fledged assistant governors. My posting was to Her Majesty's

Prison Holloway — the mecca of the women's service. My first position was to be the assistant governor in charge of the Borstal Recall Wing, responsible for girls who had been recalled to borstal under the terms of their licence.

D Wing — 'Opera box lobbies with an infinity of little doors'
(see page 33)

CHAPTER 2

'Nicks' for Women 1970 — 1977

Just 15 years before I joined the service, Ruth Ellis was hanged in Holloway Prison for killing her lover, David Blakeley. She was the last woman to be hanged in the UK—on 19 July 1955. Her death had a devastating impact on many of the prison staff and particularly those who had been detailed for condemned cell duty. Some would talk about this event, others not. Some were severely traumatised.

Just ten years before, women prisoners could be given up to three days on bread and water for breaking prison rules.

Many of the officers and assistant governors I worked with in the 1970s remembered these events quite vividly. As did some prisoners.

Nelly, an 'old lag' wrote about her 'service' at Holloway and Strangeways, Manchester in the 1940s in a wing magazine.

> In my many years of service in Holloway and other HM establishments, I can now look back with amusement upon several, if not many, tragic but at the same time hilariously funny incidents.

> One......took place at HMP Strangeways in the late 1940's

> I'd smashed up my cell with great skill, to say nothing of dexterity, having previously received verbal tuition on how to do same from some of my fellow compatriots. When the officers arrived to remove me from the scene of the crime, I felt that I should add the necessary finishing touch to the above mentioned smash up, and duly belted a couple of them with, to boot, a prison shoe, which, may I say, was on my foot.

> For my pains, to say nothing of theirs, I appeared in front of a very stern male governor, who suggested I might enjoy six days of solitary incarceration with a reduced diet—of bread and water. I did my first three days, and after a brief

respite of one day (it should have been two, but I was naughty and lost that privilege) I began on the second session, and I decided to amuse myself. Using the crusts of the four slices of bread, the middle of which I had eaten, I turned my chair upside down and began to play hoopla with the said crusts. My keeper, who solicitously scrutinised me every half hour, reported me for misuse of prison property, namely, one chair. I again appeared in front of the same very stern male governor who gave me a further fourteen days loss of privileges, which included loss of the said chair.

The women's prison service I joined was very different. Capital punishment had been removed from the statute book in 1965. Bread and water wasn't a punishment option; the daily regime in women's prisons had changed dramatically under the leadership of two enlightened and courageous female governors who eventually won the argument with the male prison service hierarchy for women to be treated differently from their male counterparts. One of their great triumphs was the abolition of the compulsory prison uniform.

Sadly and unbelievably not all change is permanent. Just 20 years or so after I left the service, in 1994, a woman prisoner was chained by her arms to her bed whilst giving birth in an NHS hospital. Surely a cruelty to match the worst in the history of Holloway and the women's service.

In England and Wales in the 1970s there were four main prisons for adult women, two borstals for girls and three remand centres with facilities for females. The number of women and girls in custody at any one time was about 1,100 against a male prison population of around 40,000. Today, in 2014 the population is around 84,500 with an average of 4000 women in custody, about five per cent of the prison population.

I have described Bullwood Hall in *Chapter 1* and I want to describe Holloway Prison as it I saw it in the 1970s. I mention most of the other women's prisons of the time just briefly, because they provide the background for the writings of the women who sent letters to me. The physical facilities, positive aspects and limitations of these institutions affected the lives of inmates and staff alike.

THE CITY PRISON, Holloway, a castellated structure of some pretensions, was erected in 1853-5 from the designs of Mr Bunning, the City architect. Of its six wings, four are appropriated to male prisoners, one to juveniles, and another to females. Each cell is carefully ventilated, and, in the winter, warmed by steam; each cell measures 13ft. by 7. The buildings occupy ten acres of ground, and provide accommodation for 436 criminals.

Cruchley's London in 1865: A Handbook for Strangers, 1865

The Holloway Prison I knew started its life as 'the chief gaol for London and the county of Middlesex'. It was technically 'a house of correction' rather than a convict prison, housing both male and female prisoners. Charles Dickens Jr in his *Dickens's Dictionary of London* in 1879 tells us that 'It is constructed on the "panopticon principle" with six wings. It is a good specimen of the style and may be inspected by order from the Home Secretary'.

Mayhew and Binny, in their *Criminal Prisons of London 1862*, describe similar galleries in Pentonville Prison built on the same model as 'looking down a Bunch of Burlington Arcades that have been fitted up in the style of the opera box lobbies with an infinity of little doors'.

In 1903 Holloway was designated for female prisoners only, having previously housed men including several notable male prisoners, Oscar Wilde amongst them; he was held in Holloway on remand.

Outside, the prison was imposing. It was apparently modelled on Warwick Castle because the local residents at the time were not keen on having a prison in their midst. Indeed the opening ceremony was rather low key to avoid upsetting the neighbours. The foundation stone, laid in 1849, is inscribed: 'May God preserve the City of London and make this place a terror to evil doers'.

The Victorian Gothic building did have a resemblance to Warwick Castle and describing this became part of my patter for groups of visiting magistrates. Entrance was through an imposing gatehouse — into the inner yard and then another even larger gatehouse. At this time the entrance was flanked by two huge carved stone heraldic winged griffins, both with key and shackles, representing the City of London; then you passed through huge wooden doors into the main hallway, up the long wide staircase to the first floor. Immediately on the right was the Governor's office and over on the left, the General Office. Beyond the Governor's office was the Board Room where all senior staff had coffee every morning after the Governor's meeting. A pair of grey glazed locked double doors a few yards further on led to the Centre. This was the hub of the prison—the link to all area—a busy area, where the life of the prison was regulated by supervising senior prison officers. Here the chief officer had her office. Most importantly all keys were kept here in a large steel cupboard, supervised by a principal or senior officer. These officers were responsible for giving out and collecting in sets of keys. Each member of staff had their own numbered set—arranged in order of seniority, hanging in rows in the steel-doored key safe. Keys were large and well-worn; cell keys rather like old church door keys—and the more modern 'pass' keys which opened connecting doors. Staff asked for their keys by number. Mine were number seven.

In the middle of the Centre with its red lino floor stood a circular antique table normally adorned with a bowl of fresh flowers; the table was polished daily by a red band—a trusted prisoner. On the other side of the Centre, a cast iron spiral staircase led up to the floors above.

By 1970 the four radial arms of the prison had been blocked off nearest the Centre. This meant that it was not possible to see down the length of each wing. No longer could they be compared to the Burlington Arcade and opera galleries. Each four story radial arm had been divided into two horizontally giving two 'wings' in each arm, one under the other. The Anglican chapel led off the Centre immediately above the entrance to the Centre. In the 1970s Holloway had six wings: D Wing for long termers and lifers, E Wing for women serving shorter prison terms, C Wing housed remand prisoners i.e. women who were awaiting trial or sentence, the C1s made up the hospital, F wing was the 'local' prison for sentenced women who came from the London area and the D1s which was the punishment or segregation unit. In addition there was a reception block, bath house, an Education Centre, offices for the Probation and After Care Service, factories, workrooms, the main kitchen, visits areas, maintenance and stores. Separate buildings outwith the radial prison but adjacent to it housed the Mother and Baby Unit and DX, the Borstal Recall Unit.

The prison had not changed that much since it was built 170 years before. Cells were still the same size. My office on D Wing was a cell, 13ft long,

7ft wide and 9ft high. I came to appreciate the size of these Victorian cells when I went to Bullwood which was opened in 1974 and Durham Prison, built in 1810 to house military prisoners during the Napoleonic wars. Both these institutions had much smaller cells which could be claustrophobic.

The cell doors I knew at Holloway were made of solid wood, sometimes clad in metal. Where these had not been 'modernised' they had a small trap door through which items could be passed, with a spy hole through which officers could observe prisoners at any time of the day or night. Electric light had replaced the old gas jets, with the switch outside the door. Each cell was furnished with an iron bedstead, a small wooden table, chair and side unit in which clothes and personal items could be stored. Two brown blankets, sheets and a pillow completed the furnishings. Unless of course the cell belonged to a long term prisoner — they were allowed curtains and bedspreads.

Each cell originally had a water closet or loo, fed by water pumped up by the prison treadmill. However, these were removed when treadmills were prohibited in 1898; after that prisoners had to 'slop-out' every morning. This was a particularly degrading system and I was always amazed at how clean the women kept their rooms, the loos and wash areas (albeit sometimes with a little prompting). The Remand Wing sometimes had problems because there was little incentive to keep the place clean when prisoners thought they might not be coming back after a court appearance.

The cell windows were depressing iron frames, made up of tiny panes of thick glass — difficult to break, small and high up on the outside wall. Too high to see anything other than a handkerchief of sky. Windows had little hinged grills which could be opened for ventilation but small enough to prevent prisoners putting their heads out. This didn't stop the women swinging lengths of wool or string (if they could get hold of either) between windows so that they could pass items and letters between cells. The grills also allowed them to post 'parcels' out of the windows. 'Parcels' was a popular method of disposing of faeces if a woman had to use her pot during the night. Disgusting for the yard party to clean up in the morning but I couldn't blame the women.

Pictures of the old Holloway show a grim forbidding place. Most of the photographs are black and white, taken by photographers who appeared to want to convey a sinister image of the prison. Yes — it was dark, grey and ominous. But hidden within the old walls were pockets of light and hope. Some women created cheerful personal worlds for themselves within their cells, particularly those occupied by sentenced women. Bright curtains and blankets; pictures cut out from magazines, calendars and photographs. Talc tins, facecream pots and shampoo bottles served as bright ornaments, often placed on crotched mats. Radios and record players blared away. However, for those on remand, cells were not long term 'homes'. Many of these women did not know how long they would be on remand nor always if they would be convicted and, if so, whether they would receive a custodial sentence. Those on remand for serious crimes where the outcomes were more predictable, made more effort with their cells but even they knew that when sentenced they would not remain on the Remand Wing anyway. There was little point in creating personal space.

Cells on the Remand Wing accommodated two or three prisoners. Sharing a cell was not to everyone's liking and making sure that peace reigned and everyone was safe was a major challenge for the wing officers. The Remand Wing had an air of impermanence and transit, fear and hopelessness. This wing probably fitted most people's idea of prison. In contrast, most wing offices, the Education Department, the Mother and Baby Unit and the chapels generated light and hope for many. The jam factory, workrooms, the laundry and the kitchens were hives of activity where staff and women bustled about the normal activities of the day. The facilities were not good; rats and cockroaches held sway and work parties fought a losing battle to keep the place clean.

Prisoners' reactions to Holloway were varied. Amazingly, some were quite positive — even a hundred years ago. Trevor May, in his *Victorian and Edwardian Prisons*, quotes a prisoner saying to the first lady inspector of prisons, 'Here I can have a room to myself, and what with three meals a day, and a doctor whenever I want him, I'm better off here' — referring to the workhouse.

The women I knew were not always quite so enthusiastic although many did appreciate the space and time they had to themselves. Jane wrote to me:

Being in here has given me time to think about my life. When I am locked in at night. I miss my family so much—particularly Ann. It seems its only when I am away from them in here that I can see how lucky I am.

Nelly the 'old lag' continued her letter in the wing magazine:

All that was a very long time ago, and a lot of water has run under the bridge since then. This last sentence has had a profound effect on me, so that I can now laugh at myself without bitterness or without feeling that I want to get even with people. I also found I could, after a great deal of deep thinking, accept truths about myself which were not initially acceptable because honesty is not flowered with fantasy. I feel that this could be a good base upon which to stabilise myself and eventually laugh at and enjoy the good things in life which don't really cost anything.

Holloway housed all manner of women sentenced for every crime imaginable. Thieves, prostitutes, murderers, con artists, thugs and bullies, terrorists, drug addicts, the mentally-ill and depressed, the inadequate and troubled, and even the innocent. For some, Holloway provided temporary 'lodgings'—where they lived whilst on remand waiting for trial. For others it was a place of transit pending allocation to a prison nearer their home. For many, it was to be 'home' for years as they served their sentence. This could be decades—the awful reality of long sentences. In ten years I had enjoyed the stimulation of school, three years in Hereford, two years in Africa, supply teaching, time at Bullwood and Wakefield and numerous other challenging experiences. Ten enjoyable Christmases. The woman in front of me had spent every day of those ten years here in Holloway prison. Ten Christmases away from her family. For most women, losing their liberty was a powerful punishment, and one which should never be underestimated.

On the whole women accepted their sentences and behaved well. Some caused serious trouble for themselves and others. The saddest were those who harmed themselves, 'lost it', 'cut up', smashed up their cells and destroyed their possessions.

Again, some things hadn't changed. Trevor May, in *Victorian and Edwardian Prisons*, quotes the Report of the Directors of Prisons, 1853: 'The strains of imprisonment made women prisoners prone to self-harm, and to what was generally known as 'breaking out', or exhibiting riotous behaviour, amounting almost to a frenzy, smashing up their windows, tearing up their clothes, destroying every useful article within their reach, generally yelling, shouting or singing as if they were maniacs'.

Violent women who destroyed their clothes were sometimes restrained by a canvas dress not dissimilar to a straitjacket. I remember placing a young woman in such a garment on the medical officers instructions not long after I arrived at Holloway. She had been flinging herself around her cell in the hospital wing, shrieking, tearing and scratching at herself with her nails. She was covered in blood. With some difficulty officers, nurses and I dressed her in the restraint. This particular garment came down just below her waist. The ends of the sleeves had long straps which buckled round her to prevent her using her arms. Fee, as she was called, was beyond all reason. She had had a calming injection which had had no effect so a 'straitjacket' was next. We needed something to break Fee's frenzied, self-destructive behaviour. Yes — it was a fight. This was my first and last experience of this restraint. I never wanted to use one again although I understood why it had been ordered. And yes — it did the job. But I found it upsetting, the more so because I was only there to 'supervise', because the hospital assistant governor was away. I had no opportunity to see this sad, mentally-ill young woman when she had regained some self-control.

This kind of disturbed behaviour was common in parts of Holloway in the 1970s and, judging by a TV programme on Holloway, in 2009. Research published in December 2013 suggests that women prisoners self-harm more often than male prisoners. It is remand (i.e. un-sentenced) and life-sentenced women prisoners who are more likely to harm themselves. We have not come far in 150 years of the modern Prison Service.

I and many of my colleagues liked the old prison. There was a lot wrong with it but it had some excellent features which the new prisons do not have. Relatively large cells with reasonably high ceilings for a start. Many older prisons are far less claustrophobic than newer ones. The old Holloway had personality. It held a sense of history, albeit much of it tragic. It represented a long penal history — capital punishment, suffragettes, forced feeding, spies, notorious women, prostitutes and the everyday petty criminal.

Her Majesty's Prison Holloway, this proud rat and cockroach infested old building was deemed unsuitable as a modern prison as early as 1930 and a new building was designed in the 1960s under the leadership of the assistant director in charge of women and girls, Mrs Joanna Kelley. Demolition started, area by area, in 1971. The first brick to fall was presented to the Governor of the day, Mrs Dorothy Wing, who had it mounted on a stand in her office. The new Holloway Prison was rebuilt over the next ten years.

During my time in the service I did not work in any of the other adult female establishments although I visited all of them. Colleagues were posted there as assistant governors and women wrote to me from these prisons. HMP Styal, near Wilmslow in Cheshire, was a semi-secure prison for women opened in 1962. It was converted from a complex of cottage homes, previously a children's home. The regime at Styal was considered quite tough even by staff from other prisons. Miss MacWilliam, its founding Governor ran a tight ship and stood no nonsense. However, for some it didn't deserve its reputation.

Women from D Wing were often transferred to other prisons to be nearer their families or because they were ready for an open prison environment. Maureen wrote,

I'm on Fox House (one of the Star Houses) Its not bad.

Another woman, Mary commented:

I hope the girls are alright and I miss them, especially Fiona. I can't write to Fiona as you aren't allowed to write to another girl in prison so will you tell her that I send my love and ask her to be good. It isn't as bad here as I thought it would be in fact it's clean and most of the girls are friendly. I can see now that it wasn't worth the barricade or the punishment that came after, but I wish that Fiona were here too.

Women did get into trouble:

I hope all the girls on the wing are being good and keeping out of trouble. I was in a bit of bother with Miss Macwilliam, the Governor on Saturday but it is alright now but I cant bring myself to apologise to her even though I know that I was very rude.

Others hated the regime:

> I am extremely unhappy here at Styal, as this place is for people whose minds
> have gone to roost. When I spoke of our parties, our sports team, our groups,
> the magazine, our choir, I was looked at in awe, as such things were never heard
> of here. During my first week, I heard a record on the community radio (private
> ones only allowed to LTIs [long term inmates]) and dared to raise my hands in a
> dancing gesture I was promptly stopped by a girl who confided that dancing was
> never allowed. On investigation, my worst fears were confirmed.

There were three other major establishments for women and in 1974 a
men's prison, HMP Drake Hall, became a women's establishment. HMP
Moor Court was an open prison, originally a private house adapted by the
Prison Department and opened just after the Second World War. HM Prison
Askham Grange and HM Borstal East Sutton Park, were also originally
private houses, the former converted into an open prison in 1947, and the
latter, opened in 1946, as an open borstal.

In 1970 the women's service was managed separately within the overall
Prison Department. Mrs Joanna Kelley was the assistant director, and head
of Prison Department P4; all the female establishments came under her
jurisdiction. My colleagues tell me that the Home Office (then the relevant
government department) paid little real attention to the women's service
with the result that Mrs Kelley made all the decisions and the women's
service was run rather like a personal fiefdom. It was her persistence and
drive that brought down the old Holloway Prison and replaced it with the
modern purpose-built new one. There are of course differing views about the
appropriateness of this decision and the suitability of the then new prison.

Personal fiefdoms no longer exist. Today's Prison Service is run on modern
management lines. I doubt that the experiences I had could happen today.
'More's the pity' one might say — others — 'Thank heavens!'

This was to be my world for the next seven years. Years of real happiness,
of despair and frustration, of physical danger, of caring and positive environments. I had no idea how it would all pan out.

CHAPTER 3

Women's Voices

Most women committed to prison in the 1970s were not serious hardened criminals. Many were tortured souls. In the main they were women who had chosen the wrong way to deal with their problems. 'Chosen' is the wrong word. In my experience most of them didn't *choose* their actions — they reacted, over-reacted and responded instinctively to situations — without thought of consequences. Many were deeply disturbed with serious mental health problems. Others were persistent petty criminals and quite a few were prostitutes. A small group had been convicted of murder — often of a husband or partner. A tiny number were imprisoned for offences against children. Some were sentenced for alcohol and drug offences or violent crime. I believed then and I still believe that many of these women had been unable to deal with their situation, their anger and frustrations in constructive ways. Many of them faced huge difficulties but had few personal resources to solve them — they were neither emotionally, educationally, intellectually, financially or socially strong. Of course, some women did make the wrong choice knowingly and, as a result, found themselves imprisoned. These were often the more sophisticated, literate and articulate women. And one or two others were just persistent criminals.

Was Holloway Prison a place for 'evil doers'? At 25 I wasn't much fussed about evil. I didn't and don't believe in the medieval understanding of the word — as 'of the devil'. 'Evil' means 'the absence of good' (as defined in the *Oxford English Dictionary*). I cannot describe any individual as evil but their behaviour may indeed be evil. I recognise that many people may disagree with me, preferring to see people who commit serious crimes as totally devoid of all 'goodness', as people who can never achieve any status other than 'bad' or 'evil'. Here I may stray into the realms of original sin. 'Life' happens to children — circumstance, culture and environment shape each child. Genes and nature play their part. As they develop into adulthood they have free will thrust upon them. They must choose their own path but that choice can become seriously skewed by the strength of the influences on their lives and indeed by the influence of their genes. Most of the prisoners I knew appeared to have a choice, on the face of it. They did not have to commit their offence. They chose to do so, but I am convinced that many just reacted to circumstances in which they found themselves. To me and others these choices were often inexplicable but that did not mean that the women were evil. A few with serious mental health problems did not have choice as we might define this.

Women didn't wear prison uniform although some items were still available—dungarees for dirty work on the bins or in the gardens for example but most of the time women wore their own clothes. This meant that for me the women looked quite normal and it wasn't always easy to imagine them committing the crimes for which they had been imprisoned.

Both women and borstal girls treated me with respect, kindness and care most of the time. Yes, tempers flared on both sides (I regret to say that a number of letters I have refer to my own temper). Some women had serious mental health problems and therefore staff expected and dealt with this kind of behaviour. This appeared to be particularly true of borstal girls who frequently smashed up their cells, cut themselves or gave themselves friction burns. Did we always deal with this behaviour appropriately? It depends on one's perspective and the response we offered. Drugs which would have been pre-prescribed for use when needed, the segregation unit, a padded cell which could only be used with the consent of the medical officer or the Governor—after talking to the assistant governor. Yes—we had options. As an inmate being given drugs to calm you down may or may not have been appropriate depending on how you were feeling. The 'liquid cosh' provided oblivion in the short term and a 'buzz' to boot. It changed nothing. Everything was still the same next day but it did create 'space' for a rethink.

Just occasionally, and only for a tiny minority of officers waiting to go off duty, an injection resolved the situation quickly. For governor grade staff, concerned with the overall management of the wing as well as the care of each individual inmate, the use of drugs or removal to the punishment unit freed up staff which benefited other prisoners. For example, inmates could come out of their cells for recreation. Talking was good and more often than not met a desperate need—and it gave the staff a real sense of job satisfaction. But needy women had an insatiable appetite for attention and talking. Rewarding bad behaviour with something a borstal girl wanted — being out of her cell to talk to the assistant governor for example, could mean that staff had been manipulated. All in all a no win situation. The secret of course was spotting trouble brewing and preventing it. Not always easy with limited resources. It was all a matter of judgement.

Prison is not an enjoyable experience although many prisoners did appear to enjoy and appreciate elements of their experience. Many of the youngsters saw it as a place of safety and a haven from the demands of an unsympathetic difficult environment — both at home and in their communities. Inside, they knew exactly where they stood. The rules were clear, everyone knew their place, the food was palatable and the beds were clean. And there was always someone to talk to. Many youngsters felt their officers were good friends — and of course there were the other inmates. But even this positive has a flipside. Jane had served a borstal sentence, been recalled and released again, re-offended and found herself in prison in November 1972:

> When I get out of here I'm really going to try hard to get a job and stick it for as long as I can. I've made my mind up this time. Prison isn't like Borstal Recall.
>
> When I left Recall I felt lost because I couldn't speak to anyone. I use to talk to you and the other officers. I think that's why I got into trouble. (I really am mad)
>
> I'm glad I'll be out for Christmas this year although last Christmas was the best one I've ever had.

Violet wrote to me from Holloway in 1974. She had served three years of a long sentence and wrote much more philosophically:

> What I meant by declining to talk of 'world affairs' was in the sense of creating divisions — between people. What is the purpose of abstracting principles, however good if those principles reinforce differences? There are sufficient similarities/compatibilities between us all to serve as natural harmony. The more important difference, for example, jobs, opinions, appearance become remote, the more remote, the more abstract those principles become. And so the chance, the way of realizing them remains obscure.

When I first came to Prison, out of fear and self-defence, the keys, the rules, the negative aspects blocked my mind to the understanding that functional symbols are no more than what they are. i.e a Rose is a Rose; a Key is a Key. As time passes by, I no longer wish or see any purpose in blaming anyone, other than myself, for having arrived here.

Do you agree that the only person who can accept responsibility for one's actions is oneself? And if one feels disquieted, troubled inside by one's actions, then one must strive to resolve the trouble...

...I hope you don't mind this rambling—I just wanted to convey to you that I feel much saner these days and I still maintain that the last three years, which is the length of time I have been here, for all the despair and inner struggle, have been the most valuable, the richest years of my life so far. I've just thought of the countless Prison 'tracks' that have been written. I haven't found one yet that has not emerged as a tragedy. This is such a pity as it only increases bitterness—the fast road to corrosion. Whilst there is another sunrise there is another day!

Violet was able to work her thoughts and ideas through on an intellectual and emotional level. Jane needed time to develop some understanding of her situation.

Not all prisoners enjoyed a positive experience and prison experiences were not positive all the time.

'Out at Last' was written for the wing magazine, a magazine I encouraged the women on D Wing to launch in 1973. The writer was a young woman who had been discharged from Holloway; she was writing shortly after her release.

Eight a.m on a cold windy morning, the gates of Holloway bang behind me. Walking away quickly without turning back for a last look. Thats what people inside tell you. Don't look back because its unlucky. The 1st February 1972, just another cold winter morning to everyone else I pass by, but it's a great day, my first day outside for 12 months.

I make my way to the nearest café, my mouth watering at the thought of eating some good food. I order the best on the menu and settle down to eat the best breakfast ever. I was not worried about how much it would cost me; after all I was rich, didn't I have in my pocket the £4 Discharge Grant I was entitled to?

Hot coffee is brought, and I sit back, and my mind goes back over the past year. It wasn't easy in prison. I never thought it would be, and yet I had come away feeling empty and numb inside. I was classed as a petty criminal, so my status in prison was not a high one. I had no great crime to boast about, no money to show for it. This in fact makes one feel a little ashamed when one is thrown into prison with various other types of criminal.

Prison is one big fight to retain ones identity, running, stumbling, holding onto the last of oneself. Many times a cry for help is heard, and more often than not, ignored. A cry for help is done in many ways, according to the person uttering it. This cry is first heard before reaching prison. By oneself becoming different, being anti-social, but who care, who helps?

All people in prison have a favourite time of day; for some it will be letters received, or visits at weekend. For me it was evening 8pm locking in time. Now I could be alone with my thoughts. No-one shouting orders, now I could be a real person. Often as I lay on my bed waiting for my medicine to work, I tried very hard to escape in my mind from the prison I lay in. I used to get very depressed, and these depressions would result in me smashing up my cell and cutting my arms. I was removed to the observation cells, and given medicine to shut me up.

Nearly 40 years on I find this difficult to read. I did not know the writer — she had been discharged before I arrived on D Wing. I did care and I tried not to ignore the cries. But who am I to say if my responses were adequate.

Prisons, like all institutions, house a number of different cultures. Prisoners have their culture, officers and governor grades theirs — to identify but three. All have common elements but each is viewed from a different perspective. Inmate culture is rough and tough even in a female establishment. Women in the same peer group could be loyal to some of their friends and cruel to others. The tone was set by the strong personalities on the wing; it depended on how they saw themselves. Did they want to be a 'baron' controlling the wing or would they use their personality in a more constructive way? Would they look out for others or quickly identify and exploit the personal weaknesses of their fellows? As on the outside some women got on together, others didn't.

Keeping one's temper and controlling frustration against the pointlessness of a sentence wasn't always easy even for the most disciplined and self-controlled women. Delia expressed her frustration to me in a letter:

> I've just started a computer course, catching up on my typing speed again and of course I'm still keeping up my other studies in drugs, shoplifting, GBH etc but I'm still sticking to my first love and applying for a job as a security adviser to the government as I feel they need one.

Not everyone liked talking. Some felt unable to express themselves well.

Dear Miss K

I hope you will excuse me writing this but I believe in fairness to you there are one or two things that I should explain to you.

I had a happy childhood until my mother died when I was aged twelve, my father unfortunately took to drink for a period of three years, during which time I lived with my sister. I had a job which I liked, but my sister had three children rather quickly and I had to stay home from work to mind them. I was only allowed to go out in the evenings when it suited my brother in law which wasn't very often. I met my husband when I was fifteen, he was home on leave from the army he went abroad for three and half years and within six months of him coming home we were engaged and married. I have often wondered if I did this to escape the life I had. I sincerely hope not.

I like to think we had a reasonable happy marriage which thank God lasted nearly twenty years. We had had rows the same as everyone, but you never saw my husband without me and the children or vice versa. The only thing was I couldn't hold on to all I had. I got deeply into debt. When my father approached my husband about it my husband just buried his head deeper in the sand. He just didn't want to know. Please don't get me wrong I am not blaming him in any way. He was always a marvellous husband and father. He just didn't want any responsibility as far as money was concerned. I tried to get out of debt but I'm afraid I just got deeper in the mire. My husband no doubt stood it as long as he could and when he met this girl at the hospital he took the opportunity and went. I can't say I really blame him. Without his wage things went from bad to worse. Within three years of each other my eldest daughter was married and my younger son joined the army. They both wanted to postpone these things but God knows I had caused enough trouble in my life without having this on my conscience. It meant I had to fit the two of them out from top to toe. I didn't want them to be different to anyone else. The answer to this was I was in the hands of the money lender and he had my Social Security book for weeks to pay him what I owed him. And of course I didn't have any means of income apart from this so it means that of course I was borrowing money from him just to live on. The outcome of it all was my husband was still having his mail sent to my house and his packs of twenty four giros were coming there at intervals. I rang him and asked him to stop them coming but he didn't and in temper I kept the one pack back in June last year. I can honestly say I didn't have any intention of drawing them and it wasn't until 13 October that I did so. Altogether I had over £400 from his account and I very kindly gave over £260 to other people to help them pay off rent areas so that you can see that I must have something lacking to have done something so stupid as I knew I was sure to get caught. It is just that I cannot refuse anyone anything, even though I know I am going to get into trouble.

Since I have been here my children visit my husband and it seems as if they are all on the best of terms. So I think it would be far kinder for me to leave things as they are and stay away from Newcastle altogether. If I go back to my children they are going to be torn in both ways and after being away for twelve months I don't feel I have the right to do this. You say I won't let anyone do anything for me , but don't you see Miss K, perhaps if they knew the type of person I am, they would have different views altogether and I don't want to become a bother to anyone as I always cause trouble whatever I do. But I would like to say that I have only met help and kindness from everyone since I have been at Holloway. It is just that I don't think I am the right person to receive it. If it is at all possible I would like to see Dr Brown to see if he thinks there is any hope for me when I go home. Personally I don't think so. I had to write this as I am hopeless trying to explain to anyone face to face. I felt you had a right to know as you have been so understanding and I would like to say most sincerely how much I appreciate it. Very many thanks.

Lucy

Lucy would have been over 50. She was persistently violent, drunk and disorderly and, after a number of non-custodial sentences, the court eventually gave her a prison sentence. Whilst in prison she was well-behaved and got on well with her fellow inmates and staff. I wouldn't go so far as to say she enjoyed her sentence but she had people who listened to her and treated her with respect. Her life was ordered and she was able to manage her temper without too many mishaps. Lucy served her time and was released; she wrote both to me and to the probation officer who had worked with her in Holloway on a regular basis. Unfortunately, things didn't go well for Lucy and she found herself on remand again.

> …I am lucky enough to be in a Portakabin with a nice set of girls and I think that counts for a lot don't you? I wouldn't say that I did it on purpose Miss K, but I am very glad it has happened because the life I was leading just wasn't me. I had really come to the end of my tether with one thing and another and I don't think I could have stood much more of Jim. Otherwise I may have been here for something a lot more serious so perhaps it's all for the best.

Did we fail Lucy? In some respects I am sure we did. Lucy re-offended and came back. But maybe she needed to come back again? We all learn behaviours that get us what we want. For 50 years Lucy achieved some kind of recognition through behaviours that were unacceptable to most people. She had huge problems with her relationships—with her husband and with her children. Being noticed and respected is important for everyone—even getting noticed in a rather negative way is still *notice*. Drunk, violent behaviour certainly brought Lucy lots of attention. People listened to Lucy in prison. Officers sat and talked to inmates on a regular basis out on the wing talking to anyone who wanted to talk whilst keeping a weather eye on what was going on around them. Probation officers, based within the prison, each had a caseload and spent time with their clients on a regular basis. D Wing had a great team of prison visitors called the Cameron Group visiting the wing. They listened. I listened. Governor grades worked split shifts and I spent virtually every evening talking to inmates. They would book up to talk and, when I wasn't in my office talking, I was talking to women in their cells.

Sometimes it wasn't easy for women to talk about themselves. Occasionally they would write to me after we had talked, as Lucy did. I like to think the story had a happy ending. I have many letters from Lucy from inside and outside prison. The last time I met her was at her home with her children and grandchildren, who had all come to meet me. The last letter I had from her was in January 1993 in which she gave me news of all her family, where they were in the world and what they were doing. The writing was shaky but clear. Sadly I didn't hear from her again. We'd known each other for 20 years. It was a long hard road for her but I like to think she made it in the end.

I believe that a custodial sentence was a devastating experience for every woman when she first came into prison. Over time, some would make the best of it and look for the positive. Others fought every inch of the way—against themselves and against the system.

Survival meant developing ways of coping with a harsh environment. My job was to create a positive environment for staff and inmates—one in which staff could help those in their care and women could help themselves. All within a secure environment and without losing one's humanity.

Asked to give a talk on prisons some time ago, one of my good friends suggested it should be called 'Screws and Nuts'. He was referring of course to the prison officers as 'screws' and the women as 'nuts'. Some women did indeed have mental health problems but certainly not all. When he talked of screws he meant of course the prison officers. Occasionally officers were called 'screws' by the women—but rarely by those serving longer term sentences. After sentence most women settled down to make the best of a bad job which included getting on with the staff.

Try this for a pub quiz question: 'What is the relationship between an arm ergometer and a prison officer?

In the 19th-century—as a punishment—male prisoners had to wind a handle on a machine which just pushed paddles through sand or water. Prison officers could tighten a screw to increase or decrease the level of resistance—making it harder or easier to turn the paddles. This kind of machine is called a crank, a form of useless labour—amazingly not removed from the statute book until 1948.

That's how prison officers came to be called screws by the criminal fraternity. Now in the 21st-century a crank machine is called an ergometer. We go down to the gym and pay to use the arm ergometer to build up our upper body strength!

The officers I worked with were never screws to me; screw is a derogatory term ill-fitting the staff. Most were professionals doing a good job in difficult circumstances. Sadly, it was only rarely that their voices were heard.

And what of these prison officers? How did their days pan out — what was it like for them working with this diverse population of incarcerated women day in day out? How did they see life in prison? I have several letters written to me by my officers which give just a brief insight into their world. What were their days like?

Usual address

18/6/73

Dear Miss Kay

At last I have found a moment to write — in fact 5.45am — before going on duty — really lovely morning — the sun brilliant — it has been very warm at the weekend — unfortunately I could not find time to sit out — I had shopping and my chores to do — it was my weekend off — my first time off since my weekend of 19 & 20 of May — so you can imagine in my room I was knee deep in dust — with the lorries passing under my window with all the rebuilding- still all neat an tidy again — (my room) — back to the grind stone today.

I put your first letter you write to the girls on the wing notice board—all were anxious to read — some have written to you — as they can with their ordinary letters if they wish- and you did have via Miss Allen — a large piece of statement paper messages from quite a few of them. I gave the paper to Bobby who kindly got it around the wing for me. Incidentally Bobby is not now a deport — and vey pleased about it — Simon and her are making plans for her release — as yet she has not heard about parole yet.

Susan's trial started Monday of last week — I believe she has written to you- I have no idea as to how long it will last — still on the prosecution — she thought it would have lasted two weeks but it will be longer than that. Lyn has her appeal today so I wonder what will happen with that — have to wait and see.

I gave out the two lots of wool on arrival and I stopped orders for the time being. I had enough else to do — hoping Miss French will commence again when she has arrived and settled in; she will arrive next week. I should have started my weeks leave then — but in fairness to her I have put it off until the following week. I am ready for my leave I must admit. I am going home to Sussex so I hope to get some nice weather and be able to sit out in the sun. Also lovely to see all my family — also my three grandchildren.

I am very pleased you liked your little gift- have you opened the bottle?

Oh I nearly forgot we have a new phone at last — for the first week you went our phone in the office was only capable of ringing and nothing more — so every time we answered the phone it was up — grab the key and dive into what was your office — so in the end I was so fed up with it — I again reported it to Mr Fellows and said that if nothing was done — I would go to the Governor — lo and behold the very next day the engineer came — phone rang and I said 'you answer it' no response — so I was very pleased and the next morning — a new phone in your office and mine so at last peace reigns.

One amusing thing last week — I was dinner patrol — (was on my own as Francis Bright had gone to Styal for the day to have a visit with her daughter).I was trying to make out the diet sheet — that day we had about 8 people coming and going for various reasons — so they had to come off lunch time's diet sheet — while working it out — I was up and down like a yo yo — either answering the doorbell or the phone — finally the phone went again — and it was the last straw — I answered in a drawn out voice 'Deeeeeeeee Wing' and at the end of the line a voice said 'Oh, I cannot remember what it was I wanted to say' My reply 'I am busy, I cannot wait for you to think' and a surprised voice said 'Oh' and I recognised it as Miss Hoover — she put the phone down — we had to laugh afterwards — but it could have been the Governor — have not heard yet what Miss Hoover phoned to say.

There I am rambling on about 'D'Wing — how are you settling in — and I bet very much different to Holloway work wise. I guess the countryside is lovely — as I assume it is in the country. One thing you have the best part of the year — you will be really settled in by the time winter arrives — may be you will be better off money wise — if nothing more. Madam Kelley came last week for inspection of the prison — no complaints re 'D'Wing — I must say the girls left rooms extra tidy — announced to them the day before that she was coming so everywhere was spotless. Nearly time to get ready to start another day — and in fact the start of 12 days and then off for 7 days.

Look after yourself — and try not to put your feet in it.

Regards
Ellen (Blackstone)

August
Dear Miss K

Thought you might like a few lines and a card just to let you know you haven't been forgotten. We hope you have settled in to your new posting and you are liking it. It must be a great change from Holloway. Everything his just normal here, organised chaos!! but we are coping under the strain.

Drop us a line if you get time as I would like to know how you are, cheerio and take care

Yours sincerely
Wendy Flight

London N6
My Dear Miss Kay

For first, sorry for the delay in answering your very welcome letter which I must say I was more than pleased to receive. How's the new place OK? You seem to be enjoying yourself at least out on the football pitch. But surely this is the season for cricket and tennis. Still I hope you are settled in alright and let me know if any-one upsets you and I'll be up there like a flash out of a gun and have em!

How's the PO behaving? All is well on D Wing at the moment. Jenny Walker is being discharged on Friday. Did you know that Susan B got her parole and is living with Sylvia. I do hope for Sylvia's sake that they make a go of it because Sylvia I think is a sincere person in a way.

The new AG started yesterday. I haven't as yet worked with her, as I have been to court everyday. As you can guess I am writing during the dinner break at Ipswich. What a case. 9 counts all to do with drugs.

Mrs Peabody is as usual working herself to a standstill with no dinner hour and no tea breaks. You know Miss Kay, I think Mrs Peabody doesn't think her staff capable. She really does do things that the staff could do.

The staff position at Holloway is really disparate at the moment. Still this week 12 POUTS started so things may be looking up.

Are you having the same glorious weather as we are down here — its absolutely baking. When are you having your holidays — do send us a card. Miss Black and her friend and my friend and I are going for a weekend in a caravan during August some time. Now if you were here we'd take you with us to do the cooking while we have a good time — how about that then. I am a very happy person at the moment how long for well your guess is as good as mine.

(THIS IS TWO DAYS F[U]RTHER ON) Sad news Jenny Walker was not discharged to-day. A lodge warrant was issued at 4pm yesterday for 28 days not paying a fine, such a shame as Jenny wrote over a month ago about this fine and was told no trace could be found. Anyway — seeing Fay outside this morning on my way out to St Albans I explained that Jenny was delayed and what had happened. She had the money so I put Mrs Peabody in the picture so what's happened now I don't know.

Norma K has gone sick. I don't think she is ill but has visitors from Ireland. She did apply for leave but as usual — no.

Well Miss Kay I'm due to go back into court any time now. The women send their regards and love. Oh yes, Emily Wilson was discharged today and Ethel came back from home leave full of drugs and is in the hospital. Freda Northwood isn't doing at all well and little Bella Brown is in outside hospital for an operation. They discovered a growth poor thing. I'm so very sorry about it.

But I really must go now the P.O. is like a cat on hot bricks you certainly must know what that means. So cheerio for now write again do its so nice to keep in touch and gear from you.

Love and best wishes
Isabel Dyer

HM Prison Holloway
August 1973
Dear Joanna

Thank you for your letter and card. I was pleased to hear that you had settled in so well until I spoke to Ben English. Imagine! Coming down and not coming to the Club for a tonic water!

We had a great time in France. Some of the wine cellars we went in were terrific, as was the wine. We saw so much it was impossible to take it all in. We had a lot of fun with the rest of the party.

Since then I have been on my summer holidays only to find that Brigitte was off sick when I got back last week. I hear from Fran Fletcher that she is very depressed with whatever she is suffering from. The only evening last week I could have visited she was not available so I haven't seen her. I sent your letter over to her and she is supposed to be writing me a note. That is all I can tell you on that score at the moment. I will let you know when 'diplomatic relations' have resumed.

Everything is happening in Holloway these days. We have started working to a Central Detail Board and it is great. I had a short day yesterday. One has to keep referring to the Board to see what one is supposed to do next. The escort board is not too bad at the moment so we are waiting till next week when the overtime agreement is to be invoked. Should be fireworks at the P.O.A meeting tomorrow evening.

We are having a farewell party for Anna Stephens next Friday evening. I was on leave the first week when Miss Norris joined us; she made a lovely birthday cake for the Unit for me.

By the way, I have been in trouble with the Governor for refusing to change my mind about not going to the Board this year. Can't be doing with it!

Lawrence plus three are a way in German camping. I do hope the weather is better there. Fiona decided not to go to Australia but I think Wanda and Jo are still toying with the idea.

This is my rest day and I am at Woodford. What a performance!! Started out with Section 60 — finished up 'unfit to plead'. She was very difficult in the dock but is now singing quietly in the cell.

Donna Moore was back to form — sick while she was on K Wing so is back on Remand. The Wing was split on Sunday. Last night the Remand side was full so the spill over had to go to the Assessment Wing. The officers on the pool are full of moans as they go from place to place. I think Molly Gill was rather sorry she asked to come off the Drug Unit. She has been in to see the Chief. Of course, all this has to be brought up when Jean is acting Chief. Stewart was back this morning and seemed on good form in Reception but I don't think she wants to know.

I always wanted to see Wigan Pier. Mary Block and I had a good laugh about it. She also wondered what the joke was about. She doesn't change. I forgot to ask Linda Lewis for your books so will try and remember when I see her.

Must close and make some tea for my singing friend, she keeps calling me 'Mam'!!

Take care and enjoy yourself. Will let you know when I can contact our mutual friend.

Lots of love
Una

Were these officers 'nuts' for working in a prison? I don't think so.

Cameo 2: A glimpse of the 'most evil woman in Britain'

She was 30 years old, about five foot six, slim, with rather broad hips. The distinctive bleached hair, so memorable in the iconic police mug-shot had gone; her hair, which was now brown was well cut and styled. She had asked to see me as her new assistant governor and stood before me dressed as fashionably as any prisoner could be. Short mini-skirt and boots. Her posture was upright and her walk easy. Four years older than me, she related to me as one young woman to another.

I got to know her well. She could be fun and had a good sense of humour. Reasonably well read, she enjoyed classical music and was interested in current affairs. She would always contribute what she could to wing activities and indeed, on occasions, would take the lead although she preferred not to increase her profile too much. She moved about the wing with confidence. Although always aware of others and potential danger, she was never cowed.

Over the years I knew her she was never subservient, but polite and respectful; always mindful of our differing roles and careful never to take any advantage.

This woman had served over six years when I arrived at Holloway. I took up my post as the assistant governor in charge of D Wing in 1972, so it was almost a year after I joined Holloway before I came into any real contact with her. I knew who she was — everyone did. I had seen her on my rounds of the prison. Everyone was aware of her presence — she was notorious. She was top of the inmate hierarchy. New prisoners wanted to see her. Many women were vociferous in their condemnation and free with their threats as to what they would do to her if they had the opportunity.

I read her record soon after joining the wing. I had to. I had to sort out in my mind how I would relate to this most notorious of women. I was shocked and horrified as I read witness statements and other trial documents. Everything I read was beyond my understanding or any experience I had had so far.

I wasn't there to judge her — that had already been done. She was sent to prison as punishment not for punishment. I wasn't God — I wasn't being asked to forgive her.

My role was clearly set out for me in the Rules for the Guidance of Prison Officers — 'For each offender is an individual — a separate and unique person. Some will be malicious, cunning and violent; some foolish and inadequate; many just ordinary people. You must learn to accept them as what they are, with calm, tolerance and humour…'.

As the Archbishop of Canterbury said, in addressing the Prison Officers Annual Conference in 1959, 'The real test of mankind and of Christians is whether they can go on loving people for what they may become, in spite of what they are now'.

I learned that there was a difference between a person and their behaviour. I remained aware of the reasons for her imprisonment throughout my relationship with her — I never condoned her actions. She was no different to any of the other women — I knew the reasons for their imprisonment but my relationships had to be based on the way we responded to one another and the way they conducted themselves in prison.

And so I met Myra Hindley — my contemporary.

A long-term prisoner's cell—'Soft furnishings' and decoration by the occupant
(see page 35)

CHAPTER 4

Cries for Help

Meg was Australian. She was a teenager — 19, vivacious and very pretty. Sadly she had come under the spell of a man much older than herself, Mike, in her home town of Sydney; he appeared to have serious delusions of his own importance and fancied himself as a 'Mr Big' in the shady world of arms dealing. As they entered the UK he was arrested by MI5. Unfortunately, Meg took it upon herself to try and 'spring him' when she went to see him in prison with a gun she had concealed on her and was promptly arrested herself. They were both designated as category A prisoners and she found herself in Holloway, on D Wing, the most secure place for her. The case was long and involved and Meg stayed on D Wing for many months waiting for her trial. This was unusual because Meg was a remand prisoner but she was a category A prisoner which required the highest level of security — D Wing. She was in a strange country without friends or family and she quite naturally found life in prison difficult at first. She missed the sun and the freedom of Australia. She came from a poor background and, as we would say today, from a dysfunctional family. She and her mother had no time for one another; her family were not really interested in her, certainly now she was in a British prison. I used to spend time with her every day — just talking. Sometime after she arrived, Meg wanted to write a book about her experiences and asked for an exercise book which I gave her; just before I left Holloway she gave it back to me and asked me to keep it for her. I am still in sporadic touch with Meg and she has given me permission to include passages from 'her book'.

Meg was completely infatuated with her boyfriend. Several women on D Wing on remand for, or convicted of, very serious offences had also fallen under similar spells with their men. To me they appeared to have surrendered their powers of judgement and had become so influenced by their menfolk that they had apparently given up their own personal values and beliefs. Prior to their involvement with these charismatic men, everything I knew about these women and their families would suggest that they would never have become involved in the crimes for which they were convicted, terrorism, murder, child abuse, firearms offences to name but a few of the usual indictments.

3 February 1973

I can't believe my luck. I've been given this to write in. Now I can go on with writing the book that Mike and I will publish one day. Everything I write or think is dedicated to my beloved husband Mike. He is presently in Brixton and fairing a lot worse than I am.

Holloway is not so bad. Well it could be a lot worse anyway. I have resigned myself to making my incarceration here a period of self improvement in many ways. I occupy myself with reading and writing. They have taken everything from me — Mike the only man I have ever loved or will ever love. I miss him so very terribly...

...They haven't been able to take my freedom of thought and my mental freedom or my self-respect away. They never will. To do so would frustrate my will, I would be as good as dead at that point. There is so much I wish to say. Mike has done so much for me, more than he ever realises. I would do anything for him. I would give my life for him, I do love him so very much. Once I thought that I would never be able to love or be loved. He has changed me in many ways. At his hands and under his influence I have flowered into womanhood. For the first time really and truly experiencing life. It seems that every time I've touched on the borders of happiness it has been pulled out like a rug from under me. And now Mike too, has been snatched away. But the difference is that we are bound together. The ties are too strong. They will never be broken. We shall be together for eternity. We have already been together since before time began. One would only be foolish to try and count the days till we are together again.

I arrived here at Holloway on the a Saturday after the previous Thursday. I am at present an unconvicted prisoner here number 9777123. My number. Mike is referred to as number 4577764; he is also an unconvicted prisoner. I know this is a ridiculous concept in itself. I have been told that the judicial system follows the adage of 'innocent until proven guilty'. If I am considered innocent then why have I been imprisoned and in solitary confinement no less? We have both been subjected to the vilest attempt at dehumanisation. My first encounter with the representatives of oppression here, sometimes referred to as the police, left me bruised, black and blue, in a state of shock...

The police have some unique means of extracting confessions. I visited Mike every day. Faithfully. To the best of my recollection I was the only visitor there every day. The first days without him were very hard. He has become so much a part of my life. I didn't know what to do at first. Our money and much of our property had been confiscated. There was a struggle to find money to live on. I can remember not eating for several days in order to keep up my visits to Brixton and take little gifts like cigarettes and fruit for Mike. I tried to do anything I could that I thought would help him feel somewhat better in that dreadful place. I cherished those visits. Being able to see, hold and kiss him even for a short while. I have not seen him now for three weeks. We are kept apart at our court appearances...

Conditions for Meg improved and she had more freedom to move around the wing unescorted. Mike wrote to her but became cool towards her.
However, she had an admirer within the police team working on her case.

14th February 1973

Valentine's Day and I am suffering the worst depression I have ever had. I got a letter from Mike that completely tore me up. A little piece of me dies every time I read it. I didn't sleep all night, was miserable all day yesterday and today. Also cried like I haven't cried in a long time. All this is why I didn't even write yesterday and I don't really feel like writing now. I just finished a letter to Mike in which I made no bones about telling him what he's done. But I really don't want to hurt him just because he's hurt me. I don't know if he is trying to chase me away but probably without realising it, he's doing a pretty good job. The one I sent was the seventh to his three. Also got sent a beautiful bunch of flowers but they weren't from Mike. That I know. HE sent them. Twice before he sent fruit. This time flowers. They made my day especially since I was feeling so miserable. In the bunch were some snow drops and I like them especially. They filled my room with their scent. I feel very flattered by whoever sent them. I'd like to know who it was. Miss K has helped me go through this. She's the only one I've had to talk to. She has devoted a lot of time to helping me get over it. Also the girls have been very nice. Loaned me a record player and radio on top of everything else.

Meg went to court every week and met Mike

3 March 1973

I have decided to return his letters for one week. Maybe he will get the message.
I have tried to tell him. I have told other people to tell him. He just can't seem
to understand what he is doing to me.

20 March

I guess I always knew what would happen. Mike sent me a telegram. It said simply
this 'I divorce thee'. That was enough I was quite upset about it at first but I realise
that it is probably the best thing that could have happened. I still love him very
much but I also feel very sorry for him. For many reasons. He really does not
understand and people don't understand him. He will probably talk himself into
Broadmoor — a prison for those deemed mentally ill.

I have a copy of just one of the letters I wrote to her after my transfer to
Hindley Borstal:

HM Borstal
Hindley
June 1973

Dear Meg

I have hopes that you will be allowed this letter although I do know that it is 'non
entitled' [Please Miss Censor?] I had hoped to hear from you but I know that
you must be having a tough time at your trial — I get reports and information
from various sources. I was a little concerned that you felt all your friends had
deserted you. This is not true Meg. I hope you know that we are all thinking
about you during this very difficult time. Perhaps it was only rumour that you felt
this? Seriously I have been most worried about things and I will be very relieved
when the outcome is known. How much longer do you think the trial will last?

    How is your back? How is the slimming going? I am most anxious to hear.
Have you heard from Bermuda Man? I do hope that he does write. Do you think
he got the letter?

Nothing particularly exciting has happened to me really. Oh yes — I was hurtling down the M6 at 70 (at least) and my windscreen shattered which was slightly unnerving — so more car trouble! It's mended now but someone said today that they thought the drive shaft was going. I do hope not.

How are your plants? Are the ferns growing? I don't suppose you have much time to look after them now. Did the mushrooms ever grow? Saw a special bucket and compost in the shops last week — a pity. Had I seen it when with you we might have tried a bucket. I am very fond of mushrooms.

I am hoping to go camping with a few of my lads soon but I have a feeling that even if I am allowed to go I won't be able to. My PO will be on a course and we are not supposed to be off together but I shall try and fix something up. I enjoy such activities as you know. May be one day you'll see England. You've a lot to see — it's not all like Holloway.

I shall finish now so that I can get this in the post then you might get it Saturday.

No one has deserted you Meg but no one can live your life for you. We are all with you in spirit if not in body — don't forget that.

Very best wishes and my thoughts are with you
JK

Meg was eventually sentenced to three years for firearms offences and served her sentence at Holloway. During that time she had no contact with her family and only from a couple of friends from home in Australia. She began to make a new life for herself in the UK — starting with friends in Holloway. She continued to write to me for sometime. I still have sporadic contact with her.

The women and girls I met in Holloway came from all walks of life and indeed all parts of the globe. Most of the borstal recall girls had pretty tough backgrounds one way and another. In the main they came from big cities and large conurbations — the north east — Newcastle, Durham and Sunderland, the North West — Liverpool and Manchester and of course London and its surrounding areas. During my training at Wakefield I had had a placement with the Bradford Family Service Unit which gave me the opportunity to visit some of the deprived areas in Bradford. This was a real eye-opener for me. I had no idea that citizens of this country could live in such run down squalid conditions. I remember that I and a colleague were asked to go and clean out a council house—social housing as it is now—in preparation for a family to move into. It was a large four bedroomed house probably built just after the war— in an appalling condition. The garden looked like a meeting place for fly tippers—rotting clothes, old cans, food waste, car tyres, old bicycles mixed up with torn lino, newspapers and broken children's toys—it was all there. Several blades of grass had struggled up between the cracks giving the pile an air of permanence. The house itself was empty. The green front door was well locked—I remember thinking that someone had fitted good new locks to a rather dilapidated door—'Necessary for keeping the squatters out,' I was told. It was the smell more than anything. Rotting and putrid. Unwashed. The house was 'empty' of furniture but almost every corner had its own pile of rags, broken plastic toys, beer cans and food cartons some with their original contents. The previous tenants had obviously had cats but no litter trays. The loo was leaking, cracked, disgusting and blocked. We did our best, cleaned-up the house as well as we could and went back to our clean beds at the staff college—only to find as we took our clothes off that we had brought back a fine selection of the local flea population. We had to go to the ambulance station to be de-fleaed and fumigated.

Houses like this were not reconditioned by the council before new tenants moved in. Some repairs were done but they appeared to take the view that there was no point in spending money they did not have on properties that would not be properly looked after.

These kinds of housing estates were home to many a borstal recall girl. Not the most brilliant start in life and it was hardly surprising that some young-sters had a really tough time. Many girls had previously been in care—taken out of appalling circumstances but left to their own devices when they reached 16. Or indeed had proved too difficult for the care system, got themselves into trouble and then been given a sentence of borstal training.

Not all had such an inauspicious start in life. A minority came from leafy suburbia and families that would often be described as 'good homes'.

Mandy Bloom was an attractive articulate, artistic and clever young woman from a 'good' background. Her parents both worked and they lived in a reasonably prosperous part of Cambridge. She had a sister who, as far as I could understand, was the complete opposite of Mandy and, consequently, drove her mad. Mandy fell prey to the local drug barons and became an enthusiastic 'pot' smoker. One drug led to another which meant she had to fund an expensive habit which she did through burglary, theft and forgery; she found herself serving a borstal sentence at Bullwood Hall, was released on licence, re-offended and came to the Borstal Recall Wing at Holloway. Mandy was fun on her good days and a real pain in the neck on her bad days! She was much at odds with herself. On the one hand she was intelligent and artistic; she wrote poetry, was articulate about her problems and had good insight into the behaviour of fellow borstal girls. On the other hand, she could be self-destructive—cutting her arms and giving herself severe friction burns; she could shout and yell and be rude and demanding.

> I wear a nylon mellow
>
> Lemon yellow nightie
>
> And I want to look in to my ear
>
> But I can't
>
> I am smoking a cigarette
>
> Thin, tobacco, hand rolled
>
> And I want to blow fire into the clouds
>
> But I can't
>
> I am dangling my fingers
>
> Over the edge of the bed
>
> And I want to put my fingers into my
>
> Yellow, thin, handmade brain
>
> But I can't.
>
> Mandy, *DX Magazine*

Staff had persuaded Mandy to take up a place at a drug rehabilitation centre on her release from Holloway. This didn't go well. Another ex-inmate was accepted on to the programme at the same time and she turned out to be a bad influence on Mandy although I suspect they were bad for each other. Together they got into a great deal of trouble, disrupted the unit and were eventually thrown out having been charged with a number of offences. Mandy was waiting for her court appearance when she wrote:

Well here I am out on bail spending Xmas with my parents. Although in theory is sounds great, it isn't I can assure you. Down one ear I've got my dad shouting his head off calling me all the whore-bags under the sun. Down the other I have my mother trying to pacify him. Yes, I do get moments of peace. Its in bed at 9.30 + lights out. Nag, nag, nag, moan, moan, moan. He won't even let me out of the house to buy a packet of cigs!!! I'm trying to drown my sorrows with a very poor edition of War and Peace. But that's so bad it makes Tolstoy's famous work sound like 'Crossroads' or in parts 'Coronation Street'! This next fortnight is going to be such an ordeal that I feel sure that I won't last it out. I've already got my passport in order for Amsterdam just in case. Yet on the other hand I'm trying to persevere; I've already written to Mrs Fritch begging another interview. I think half the problem stems from the fact that my stepfather is the only person on earth that I dare not retaliate against. Though I don't know why; I feel sure that its not fear that he would resort to physical violence. It's a bit sick though when one is classed as a slut and such like and nothing on earth will change that opinion.

Mandy became a real drug addict. She wrote to me regularly for two years after she left Holloway. During that time, she went to Amsterdam, *the* place for addicts but even there, got into a great deal of trouble as she stole to fund her habit. She became involved with a French student, became pregnant and moved to Corsica; twins arrived but sadly one died. Motherhood didn't come easily to Mandy and this together with her drug habit made life difficult for her — no money, no stability and a child to cope with. In the last letter I had from her she told me that she was contemplating having her daughter adopted.

Dear Miss Kozubska

Sorry I have taken so long to write to you but you know what I'm like when I've reached a new area. As you can see I am still in Corsica though I couldn't tell you how long I have been at this particular place because my clock as broken. You may wonder what my clock has got to do with me not knowing how long I have been here. Well, quite a lot really—I've rented an old peasant house up in the middle of the mountains and my only way of knowing the time is by looking at the sun and that is such a hassle I don't bother normally; so I don't bother counting the days either. The house is very beautiful in a simple way. Both inside and out are whitewashed and all the floors covered with earthenware tiles. I have no gas, no electricity and no running water. I cook on a open fire in the kitchen and bake in the stone oven in the garden. I see by candle light and fetch my water from the well. It all sounds very beautiful and romantic, it is—but its bloody hard work as well. But tranquillity is what I needed after 10 hectic months in Amsterdam—I am about two miles from the nearest shop and about four miles from the village. Anyway, what else is there? Pierre is out of the army and I'm expecting to see him in two weeks. Mia is staying with a Dutch couple I met in Amsterdam. You may wonder what she is doing there—well the reason is if everything falls flat with Pierre, they hope to adopt Mia. I am not sure about it yet. The problem is that I am such a restless unreliable soul that I consider it pretty stupid of me to try and convince myself that I'm capable of looking after a baby. But I am so stricken with conflicting emotions over the whole situation that I really don't know what to think anymore. I'm beginning to believe that my only reason for wanting the child back is because it's a nice ego booster and I don't for one minute believe that if I did have her back, I'd be a good influence on her at all. Being that its my duty to be a good mother then surely I should be truthful with myself? I am far too restless, impatient, unreliable, unstable, aggressive changeable etc to even cope with a baby alone. Don't get me wrong, I love Mia very much, that in fact is the reason why I am contemplating adoption. But of course if everything goes OK with Pierre then I'm hoping I may be able to cope a little better—after all a problem shared is a problem halved!! Well that's about it for now—but write soon and let me know all the news in England.

Love as ever
Mandy

I didn't hear from Mandy again.

The women I knew on D Wing in the main were my age or older. A number of them were real recidivists. Back and back they came to prison. Freddie Fielding would have been in her mid-50s. She had spent 20 years in prison on and off. She was a good looking woman, tall and always well-dressed; well-spoken and well-educated. When I met her she was serving her umpteenth sentence and was a couple of months away from her release date. Although I have no letters from her—she was above all that—she, like many of the women on the wing 'looked out for me' and made sure I didn't make too many mistakes. I owed Freddie quite a lot.

One of the inmates on the wing when I arrived was a young arrogant woman from Nigeria. She had been educated in England and spoke well. The officers had asked her do something and she had flatly refused. I was asked to go and 'sort her out'. Up I went to her cell on the upper landing. The door was open I knocked and went in. I can't remember what she had been asked to do but I do remember feeling that it wasn't unreasonable. The woman refused. I wasn't used to such a response and the more I insisted the angrier she became. I was just about to lose it—who knows what would have happened if Freddie hadn't heard the row, come in, and forcibly pushed me out of the door saying—'She is not worth it. Leave it.' I hope I wouldn't have hit the woman. Fortunately I didn't have to find out. Women like Freddie had years of experience living in prison. They saw officers and governor grades come and go, they knew the ropes and understood that a quiet wing was easier to live on than a troubled one. They could exert substantial influence over what happened on a wing, as could most personable long termers and most of them used their influence constructively, outwardly anyway.

Freddie was discharged from Holloway and found a job as a housekeeper to a rich old man. Unfortunately she got greedy and, together with an accomplice, killed him hoping to get hold of his money. She returned to Holloway to serve a life sentence. Freddie is long since dead but I shall not forget her. She made sure that a young assistant governor didn't lose her career through a thoughtless loss of control.

I am often asked how I could possibly like women who had committed heinous crimes. Myra Hindley was on D Wing throughout my time at Holloway. I got on well with her. How could I forget what she had done? I learned early on in my career that if I was to work with people who had been convicted of terrible crimes I had to separate their actions from their personalities. I liked Myra but was appalled by her offences. We talked about this many times. I met Myra seven years after she was convicted both of murder and being an accessory to murder, for which she had been given two life sentences. I met an outwardly confident but inwardly unsure woman. At the time she was coming to terms with her relationship with Ian Brady and his influence over her. In my discussions with her, although not always with others, she fully accepted her part as a willing accomplice in these most horrible offences and, as a result, had no self-respect. She told me that she had no idea why she did what she did other than she wanted to please Brady and be with him. She had been totally besotted with him. My role was not to punish her, not to find out why she did what she did but to help her live her life constructively within the prison system.

Myra returned to her Catholic faith despite opposition from the Catholic priest at Holloway. She knew she needed God's forgiveness. As far as she was concerned, she couldn't put the clock back, she couldn't undo what she had done. She had to live with it, with all that meant — particularly people's reactions to her because of her offence. In one of my last conversations with her before she died, some 30 years after our first meeting, she talked about living with what she had done. She couldn't change the past. She deeply, deeply regretted what she had done and believed that only God could forgive her. She hadn't been hanged so surely this meant she had to move on and grow as a person. She knew that others would never accept this and this was her punishment.

Loneliness besets so many of us. Looking back now, I think that many of the women who wrote to me were lonely, particularly immediately after they left prison. I had been able to talk and listen to many during their sentences but when they left, where did they go? Getting back into their relationships wasn't always easy. Time away strained things and it took time to get back to the comfortable old ways. Sometimes there just wasn't anyone to listen when they were feeling at their most vulnerable and lonely. Writing to me was one way of getting in touch with an experience which hadn't necessarily been all bad. Small acts of kindness grow in the imagination and take on much significance.

Scarborough

7.7. 1973

Dear Miss K

I am writing this at 6am — it is so wonderful to be free again, and although you have probably heard this so many times — I intend to stay this way. D wing was absolutely b—horrible after you left. Complete chaos, officers bawling, women doing the same and no Miss K to smooth thing out. Poor little Gaynor got moved to another wing and Susan walked round like a zombie. Mary was to be discharged on the same day as myself, about 6pm the previous evening Miss Leissner came and presented her with a fine or 28days. You can just imagine the effect it had. Welfare officers said they couldn't do anything etc. Quite a few of us became a bit 'awkward' shouting 'If only Miss K was here, she would sort this mess out.' Anyway I was given various phone numbers to try and get the money. Anyway everything turned out alright. I was in Reception and I heard Mary yelling 'Jo, Jo'. I am sure everyone thought she was shouting from outside on her way to work as I wasn't leaving until 9.30am. But an officer, Mrs Leaf, had gone down to the Gate and Sylvia was there to meet Mary and she paid the fine. You should have seen us, we were all laughing and crying at the same time. But what dirty pigs some police can be after Mary doing 21 months then slapping that fine in.

I myself was very lucky. A letter was forwarded to HMP from the Matron here asking if I would like to do holiday relief. Miss Fullerton allowed me to make a phone call from her office confirming that I would like to come. What a thrill making a phone call from the prison. I am here until the middle of the month and then I have another position lined up with a home for older people . Not sure of its proper name . One of the Committee members obtained it for me. It seems just like a cake walk for me cooking for 30 people instead of 300 and receiving the vast sum of £28 per week instead of the princely sum of 72½p.

I stay here most nights as it saves money travelling back and forward home. David keeps ringing to make sure I haven't gone out.

I know I very rarely showed any feeling towards you when I was on the wing with you. Maybe because I didn't want to be labelled one of your blue eyes but I really did love and respect you and the night you came to say goodbye I cried and cried which in itself was good as it released a lot of my tension.

Please write soon.

All my love

Jo

Scarborough

29.8.73

Dear Miss K

sorry for the delay in answering your letter, but I have been quite busy getting myself settled and feeling more stable. As I told you I was doing relief work for two weeks and then got a post at an Old people's Home. I started on 16th July. I like the work and get on well with other staff usually there's always one who one doesn't like , but here everyone is great, and the Matron thinks I am a marvellous cook and a great worker. I have two staff in the kitchen , a man who does the veg and cleans stoves etc and girl or should I say an young woman who is a bit thick and who drives me up the wall sometimes. But I feel sorry for her which is good as otherwise I might blow my top at her.

My family are fine. Simon went to a Billy Graham thing. Ella May is home for a couple of weeks. David is still grumpy hobbling about but he gets on well with the kids so that's great. I hope you are getting settled and it would be nice to see you again. May be we could arrange something you could come here for a visit?

You mentioned playing the tape of the Christmas Concert. Do you think you could please possible get a copy for me and post it here. I wanted to buy one on D Wing but I didn't have any money at the time until I got that tax rebate. That eventually came. I would like David and the children to hear the concert . I so enjoyed playing the piano for it. I have just been listening to Brahms 1st Piano Concerto. I must close now otherwise I will never get up in the morning. I catch the bus at 6.45 but usually get up at 5.30 and do odd jobs like letting the dog out etc. David sends his regards

All my love

Jo

PS If I write a letter to Mrs Wing and enclose it to you would you address it? Thanks.

There are so many stories behind the letters I have. Jo, Lucy, Meg, Mandy, Freddie and Myra are just a few. Myra's story continued for 37 years in all, until her death on 15 November 2002. She had planned her funeral and had invited a tiny number of people she felt were her friends, myself amongst them. Security was tight as it always had been for her, apart from one memorable day in 1973 when she and I left Holloway Prison, en route for a walk in the park.

Holloway Prison, Inner Gate (apparently inspired by Warwick Castle)

(see page 33)

CHAPTER 5

'And you the Governor shall hold.......'[1]

Myra and I walked out of the gates of Holloway Prison for that notorious outing; we walked over to the Governor's house and I gave her into the Governor's care. I remember well the enormity of what I was doing at the behest of my seniors. I was escorting the most notorious woman of the day out of the gates of Holloway prison. Myra had dressed carefully—in her best most appropriate clothes. The gate officer opened the little wicket gate in the huge main gates and we crossed the 25 yards over the cobbles to the red brick Governor's house, up the small flight of steps to the front door. The door opened almost before I knocked and we went in. I returned to the prison without my charge.

Together with the senior medical officer, Mrs Wing and Myra got in to the former's car and drove to Hampstead Heath for a walk. They were away for a couple of hours—I was in my office—the phone rang—Mrs Wing—'Would you come and pick Myra up please'. This was the first time, as far as I knew, that Myra had been outside the prison since her conviction seven years before, other than for medical or police reasons. As I gave my keys in to the officer on the Centre on the way out, I wondered what the reaction from the staff would be. It was obvious we were leaving the prison otherwise I would not have given in my keys. News travelled fast. Why this wasn't anticipated by the Governor and head office remains a mystery. The evening papers led on it and, the following morning, the national dailies shrieked the news. The furore was staggering. No one had foreseen the immense reaction or the orchestrated press campaign against Myra, the Governor and the Home Office. I couldn't believe what I read the next morning. It went on for days. After that, we all knew Myra would never be released. Myra knew then how difficult her life was going to be. She was extremely depressed in the days following this episode. I supported her as best I could. What could

1. Extract from the warrants issued by the courts giving legal authority for the prison Governor to imprison an individual.

I do or say? Writing to me a couple of days after the event:

> You have this special 'knack' of seeming to share implicitly people's sorrows and
> sadnesses, and also that of dispelling fears and anxieties...
>
> ...It isn't simply that you make me feel like a human being, but a special kind
> of one and this is true of others too, that you make them feel special...
>
> ...You have been a constant source of support and encouragement to me, and
> through you I have regained no small quantity of self-respect and self-confidence.

The newspapers, the media and public opinion would ensure that she would never be released. And she never was. It was obvious that no Home Secretary would risk his or her reputation and none ever did. It was said that Myra sold as many newspapers as Princess Diana so there were vested interests at play as well.

Mrs Wing never recovered from this event. She was 'disgraced' and retired shortly afterwards. Did she carry the can for Mrs Kelley, the person in charge of women and girls, or did she act off her own bat?

So many points of view to consider. Myra had committed a series of most heinous crimes—how could anyone imagine that she should be allowed out for 'jollies' in the park, let alone be released? Prison was 'too good for her'. In today's litigious times Myra might have had a good case against the prison authorities for exposing her to events that would damage her opportunity for release on parole. Was it a real error of someone's judgement which damaged a lifer's chances?

If we set aside the death penalty and settle for life imprisonment for serious offenders how should we treat them? Are we responsible for their mental welfare? Now, 'outside' in society, companies have a duty of care for their employees. Every organization has a duty of care for those it works with. It was different in the 1970s. We hadn't started to look at these issues. We didn't have a Human Rights Act then. And yet, now, we feel outraged when prisoners invoke those rights successfully.

Myra's life was never simple or predictable.

Everything came to light when Fiona 'grassed' on them. The escape plan was discovered. But prior to that, soap had been discovered on a set of officer's keys. Imprints had been made. Something was up. But who was the officer planning to help escape?

Pat Cairns was an officer on D Wing. Myra and Pat fell in love and laid plans to escape. I learned later that sometimes they used the cultural activities I organized as a cover for their meetings. Myra said she wanted to play the piano. I arranged for her to practice in the chapel. I took her there, locked her in and returned to pick her up at a fixed time. Pat Cairns would have been carrying out her normal wing duties and as it transpired, she would pop in to meet Myra, unsuspected by anyone. They were planning their escape.

On the face of it Myra was a model prisoner and I certainly hadn't thought that she would try to escape. It never crossed my mind. I was extremely busy trying to ensure that the women on my wing had as positive and stimulating an environment as possible and that the staff were well-led and happy. I wanted inmates to have as good a quality of life as was possible. I believed that if they had little to fight against and as much intellectual and cultural simulation as possible then they would use their energies to reflect on themselves and their behaviour rather than cook up dastardly plans. How wrong I was!

The plans came to light after I had been posted from Holloway and so I escaped much of the flak for what went on. At the time I was relieved I had avoided any censure but never bitter that I had been duped. What did I expect? I felt pretty stupid and I should have been more observant. I should have expected that a woman facing the rest of her life in prison would try and escape—and I didn't. Myra and I never discussed this episode in her life. I could have done so years later when I visited her regularly but I felt that in many ways I was to blame. I couldn't condemn her for what I felt was a natural thing to do. Had I been more vigilant and a little less trusting I might have helped Pat Cairns avoid her six year sentence. However, had my senior colleagues warned me that the officer concerned had given cause for concern previously I might have been more prepared.

Duncan Staff, a journalist, in his book on Myra Hindley, *The Lost Boy*, states that security at Holloway was lax. It is a point of view. No one escaped from within Holloway during my time there and many of us were concerned to provide a constructive atmosphere and as good a quality of life as we could in difficult circumstances.

Dear JK

After long months of silence from my end, do I need to reintroduce myself? You'll understand, of course, why I haven't written lately, so no need to go into explanation. Nor will I mention 'the case' for obvious reasons; the time will come when all will be made clear, if not fully understood. I've had a 'daffodil card' from Mrs Wing, saying how sorry she feels about the publicity etc, and that her thoughts and hopes will be for us. And at Christmas she sent me 'snowdrop card' along with a lovely letter, in which she mentioned that you'd been to lunch about a month ago (probably in Nov) and brought a beautiful poinsettia 'which flourishes', so she is not starved of flowers. So although I've apparently neglected you by not writing, I've still been hearing about you...

...I don't like it here any more. I wonder if I could be transferred to your borstal, or Brixton or the Black Hole of Calcutta, or anywhere. I think I have assumed two new statuses (there's no plural for that word according to my dictionary) that of Public Enemy No 1 (Mind you that is probably not a new status) and Chief leper Extraordinaire. It could all be in my mind of course, a figment of my imagination, a symptom of paranoia'.

Myra

Herefordshire

13.12 73

My Dear Joanna

It was kind of you to write and send the photographs — not even Armstrong Jones could flatter me although Poly Express chap once did!

Poinsettia is still a great joy and I love it very much. It was fun to see you and do come wherever you can. There has been nothing in the northern editions about Cairns and I was very sorry to hear about it. I know she was always under suspicion but after that searching VC enquiry with a QC in the chair I inclined to think it was a case of give a dog a bad name!

I've just written an innocuous Christmas letter to Myra c/o the Governor but do you think she has become a Lesbian in prison? I often though so in E Wing days when Norma was here and indeed with others. I'm not sure how Alice can be 'go between to the outside'. Is she having parole? Fond as I am of the child I know she would always be agin the government!

I certainly do not think you can expect loyalty to the system from any inmate. Equally I am certain that you get personal loyalty from them — and that is not only Holloway. — there is the well known case of the Parkhurst prisoner who gave himself up when late on parole because he couldn't let his Governor(Alistair Miller) down and the mad chap said to have been murdered by the Krays because he wouldn't let the governor of Dartmoor down. Sadly I don't think they can get beyond the personal and this is where I think we all fail. I know no way of getting them to see that the future is greater than the past!

If staff morale is low that is much more worrying. Long before I knew the service, Holloway Officers were famous for their determination to make the system work. Ever since I have known them they have been overworked and underpaid but they have been dedicated and loyal. Sometimes I used to look at some of the younger ones and wonder how they did it so cheerfully. Back at midnight from Southampton, up and away at 6am to Birmingham! They were as noble as my ATS and higher praise I could give to none. Obviously they get upset; they have boyfriend family and even girlfriend troubles and they need support but who doesn't. Occasionally there is a bad egg but that is inevitable in a large service.

I hope but don't expect you to have Christmas at home. I'm looking forward to my first selfish one for 32 years!

Anne sends love and joins with me in the hope of seeing you soon again.

Love
Dorothy Wing[2]

I never cease to be amazed when I read reports in the newspaper following a gaol break or an attempted escape. There is always an outcry — someone must be blamed and everyone appears indignant that it has happened. And indeed it is a quite serious matter when inmates succeed in escaping; escapes frequently have major consequences for the public, police and the Prison Service — not to mention the secretary of state in charge of prisons, now of course the Ministry of Justice. But *why* are we indignant? Why do

---

2.   Governor of Holloway Prison.

we think that civilian prisoners shouldn't try to escape? We are thrilled when members of the armed services escape during wartime and we watch films such a *Colditz* with enthusiasm. We are filled with admiration when a hostage manages to outwit his captors and escape. The courage, ingenuity and patience needed to escape from captivity is considerable. People convicted of crime do not lose their burning desire to be free, to lead their own lives again. We must *expect* prisoners to try and escape. The trick is to create as stimulating and constructive an environment as possible but at the same time put all the necessary security provision in place, the latter depending on the degree of risk associated with each prisoner. This is the part I didn't get right. On the whole the prison service does this well and statistically escapes from prison are insignificant. This was also true in the 1970s.

Escapes can have their funny side. Whilst at Bullwood Hall, as a temporary officer prior to my going to Wakefield for my staff course, I was involved with two abscondings. Girls were often taken out of the borstal to help at local events. One beautiful day in the summer of 1970 we took a group of girls to the local fête to help out. Marina, from a well to do family, offered to help with the pony rides. And help she did. In a quiet moment she selected the best looking mount, leapt on and spurred her way to freedom!

Extract from a press clipping from 1970:

BIG POLICE HUNT AS ESSEX BORSTAL GIRL FLEES

A NATIONWIDE alert went out to police today to look for an 18 year old girl who escaped from a Borstal working party. The girl, Susan Phillips, was one of four who ran away from Bullwood Hall Girls Borstal, Hockley. Susan escaped from a group helping with the preparations for a gymkhana.

A number of girls worked on the farm party at Bullwood Hall—they looked after the grounds and did some gardening—supervised by an officer of course. Girls were only put onto the farm party if staff felt they could be trusted. One summer's evening, Pat Bartholomew, a borstal officer and I were driving past a field of maize on our way out for a drink. Suddenly, three faces popped out of the maze—looking up and down the road. We screeched to a halt—the girls had absconded from the farm party that morning. *Of course* they would give themselves up to us — but we shouted their names in vain. We drove on to phone the police and the borstal — no mobile phones in those days. Returning to the scene we waited for the police to arrive which they did — in force, followed by staff from Bullwood. Searching a maize field without a helicopter isn't easy and needless to say it wasn't a successful search. The police had brought dogs with them and told us that on no account should we run otherwise the dogs would chase us. Unfortunately, one of our number didn't heed this advice and ran for some reason. The dogs gave chase, caught her and had her pinned down in a ditch! All this provided much amusement and a great distraction — the girls got away. They were picked up some days later having enjoyed their jaunt immensely. On the quiet we too enjoyed ours — perhaps at our colleague's expense.

Planning to escape — escaping — is not deviant behaviour — it is normal. Prison staff have a duty to protect the public and to prevent inmates from getting themselves into more trouble. But prison staff have a responsibility to create constructive environments in which those in their care can start to sort themselves out. It is a balancing act.

Security preyed on everyone's mind at some point or another.

How I wish I could tell Mike all the things I have seen and lived and I am sure he has much to tell me. But all the mail is censored. They suppress the truth about these places and the conditions herein. I have learned a variety of things since my arrival here. One is not to request medical attention and the other things is that the rules and regulations change to suit the moods of my captors. At my reception into this institution of higher learning, I was classed as Category A, a special prisoner. The only woman in this resort to fall into this category, otherwise considered highly, potentially dangerous. Me. My confinement is solitary and I am locked in my 'room' for 23½ hours out of 24hours. I have manganese bars and double locks on my room and am escorted at all times by two very lovely ladies, who are part of the prison staff. I am never allowed to speak to any of the other women prisoners on the wing. I am presently on an open wing of already sentenced women. The only times I am permitted out of my 'room' are to use the facilities once or twice a day and for my exercise period of 10-15 minutes each day.

Meg wrote this in her diary. She was not the only woman category A prisoner but she was the only category A remand prisoner.

Preparing girls for release was part of borstal training. Some hadn't been outside for months and were understandably apprehensive; it was normal practice to take girls out just prior to their release. Naturally I took my turn taking borstal recall girls out. Two girls and I went to Madam Tussauds and then out for something to eat afterwards. We had enjoyed our egg and chips and the bill arrived. I had run out of cash and only had a cheque book! Cheques were not accepted in this café (no cash machines in those days and the banks closed early). I had to leave the two borstal girls as collateral and hurried out to find somewhere to cash a cheque. A shop took pity on me and I rushed back to find them still sitting there laughing their heads off.

In those days it was more acceptable to take low risks. But looking back, we were not good at assessing risk objectively.

My confidence gave me problems on a number of occasions. I felt I had excellent relationships with the women on D Wing but sometimes this confidence was rather misplaced. Two women imprisoned for drug offences were due for release and their probation officer wanted them to go to a drug rehabilitation centre. The women were prepared to consider this but they would need to spend a day at the centre to be assessed for their suitability. However, none of the D Wing officers wanted to take them because they felt that these two were escape risks. The probation officer wasn't in a position to take them. Naturally I said I would. After all they wouldn't escape from *me*, their assistant governor. Off we went—on the bus to somewhere in a London suburb. Armed with an address and a map we eventually found our way and arrived at the centre. First stop—the loo. In we all went—each into a little cubicle. I wasn't long but when I emerged they had gone.

I had to ring the Governor and tell her I'd lost two. I returned to Holloway on the bus by myself. I cannot remember ever feeling so shocked and embarrassed. The women were picked up two days later, stoned out of their minds somewhere near Piccadilly. Neither the officers nor the women on the wing were sympathetic. They all said, 'We knew they were going to run—it was obvious'. It was a hard way to learn.

Security governs prison life. How we impose that security—how we treat people within secure accommodation reflects on each one of us party to that imposition.

CHAPTER 6

Day by ...

As already outlined *Chapter 2* in Holloway Prison was a vast dilapidated old building, full of cathedral like spaces on the one hand and nooks and crannies on the other. It was both imposing and squalid. We battled furiously against invading cockroaches and rats in the kitchen and cleaning parties worked continuously to keep the dark, grubby yards clean. Each wing had washing and toilet areas—crazed old ceramic basins and lavatories with high cisterns and pull chains. The old Victorian bathhouse still functioned—a long building of half-doored cubicles, and clouds of steam reminiscent of the grand spas in towns like Harrogate. The huge old fashioned brass taps were on the outside of each cubicle so that the bathers couldn't control the temperature of the bathwater. Officers were in control but on the whole they were not unkind. The baths were large, water was plentiful; the benison of hot water helped many a woman to feel clean and refreshed in mind as well as body.

As I also noted earlier, the Victorian water closets in each cell had been taken out and replaced with the degrading and humiliating practice of slopping -out (Bullwood Hall was built without in-cell toilets). There was little that staff could do to change this. Unofficially officers would sometimes let women out of their cells to go to the loo if they knew them well and trusted them not to take advantage of the situation; particularly helpful if women were sharing a cell. However, this kindness was discretionary and staff could leave themselves open to criticism and more if anything went wrong. Fortunately, it rarely did.

Cleanliness was really important to both women and staff for obvious reasons. I have no recollection of ever having to ask women or borstal girls to wash themselves or their clothes. Each prison establishment had a laundry which did all the linen and any prison clothing in use—dresses, overalls and dungarees for example. Clouds of steam billowed from great vats in prison laundries and women allocated to work there didn't have it easy. Prisoners could send their personal laundry to be washed if they wanted to but in most cases they would do it themselves. Both Holloway and Bullwood Hall had hot pipes a plenty which doubled as 'driers' — more often than not clothes would be festooned in women's rooms. Each wing had an iron and ironing board which the women could borrow from the office if they wanted to and provided the staff considered it safe to allow a woman to use this equipment. It was rare for women to abuse these privileges but, if they did, they had to cope with the displeasure of their fellows as well as more formal consequences from the likes of me.

At the end of the 1960s Joanna Kelley, the assistant director responsible for women and girls had introduced an experiment in which women were allowed to wear their own civilian clothes. A Prison Service Circular Instruction issued in 1970 reads as follows:

WEARING OF CIVILIAN CLOTHES BY WOMEN AND GIRLS DURING SENTENCE

1. Allowing women and girls to wear civilian clothing has been very successful and it has improved morale and self-respect. This circular is to tell you that the privilege is now being put on a permanent basis and to inform you that the original arrangements notified in Circular Instruction No. 53/1968 have been revised in some respects in the light of experience. The changes are incorporated in this circular, which sets out this arrangement in full.

PROCEDURE ON RECEPTION

2. Every woman should be informed on reception that if she has suitable clothing or can arrange to have it sent in, she may wear it if she wishes. No civilian clothing may be purchased at public expense for women who will be in custody under sentence for less than 6 months.

3. A women serving 6 months or more who has insufficient clothing of her own, or who prefers not to wear her own clothing, will be provided at public expenses with such items as may be necessary to secure for her an outfit in accordance with the scale set out in paragraph 8 below. The clothing should normally be purchased for her by a member of the staff who, at the Governor's discretion, may take the woman shopping and help her choose the garments.

4. Within reason, she should be allowed to choose what clothing she wishes but if the Governor has an objection to the type of clothing chosen she should discuss the case with the Assistant Director.

5. Women and girls will be issued with prison clothing if they do not wish to take advantage of this privilege.

The circular goes on to spell out each woman's responsibility for looking after the clothes, etc.:

SCALE OF ISSUE OF CLOTHING

6. The total amount spent in providing clothing for any woman should not normally exceed £25 as it is not expected that all items in the outfit will have to be purchased. Where, exceptionally, it is necessary to purchase a complete outfit, expenditure should not exceed £30. The item comprising a complete outfit of civilian clothing and the suggested sum to be spent on each garment are as follows:

ITEM	COST PER GARMENT		
	£	s.	d.
2 skirts		1	15
or 2 prs jeans/trews...or one of each of these garments	2	0	0
2 blouses, or	1	0	0
2 dresses	2	10	0
3 pairs of stockings		5	0
And	1	0	0
2 suspender belts/roll ons/corsets			
or			
3 pairs tights		7	0
1 pair outdoor shoes	3	0	0

ITEM	COST PER GARMENT		
	£	s.	d.
1 pair indoor shoes	2	0	0
1 cardigan	2	0	0
2 brassieres		11	0
3 pairs knickers/panties		5	0
2 slips/waist slips	1	0	0
2 nightdresses	1	0	0
or	1	15	0
2 pairs pyjamas			
3 vests		5	6
2 overalls	1	5	0
6 handkerchiefs		1	6
1 plastic rain hood		1	0
1 mackintosh, nylon*	2	0	0

*Navy—light blue mackintoshes should not be purchased as there could be confusion with the blue overalls worn by officers

I don't remember plastic rain hoods being much in demand but some women did want them—to keep their hair dry if they had to walk from wing to wing for work.

Long-term women tended to have a mixture of clothing—items bought for them from the public purse and their own clothes. The length of sentence tended to determine the balance. Long term women would have one or two items of their own—a coat perhaps—or items sent in for them by their families but as the years passed, as their own clothes wore out, most of their clothing would be bought for them by staff. Again, depending on the length of their sentence, women were allowed different amounts of clothing in their rooms; they had little storage space and would have to put extra items in to their 'property'—the prison's main store for prisoners' belongings.

One of my roles as an assistant governor was to go shopping for the women when an officer could not be spared. Occasionally I would take one of the women or borstal girls with me which I always found helpful, not really having an eye for what other people wanted to wear. I had an idea about those of my own age—in their 20s and younger—but I struggled with those much older than I was. This was the age of Mary Quant, the mini-skirt and mock leather PVC. I had a rather fetching blue-pleated mini-kilt—and a dark blue blouse with a shiny PVC collar which was much admired by the women—I am not sure about the staff. Amazingly, neither the Governor nor my more senior colleagues ever made any comments about the length of my skirts but, looking back, my skirts were never of the pelmet variety. My colleagues were tolerant of me and indeed of the women's fashions.

Some of the most difficult items to buy were girdles and brassieres. There were several middle-aged and older women on D Wing who were quite firm about what they would and would not wear. Mable was well over 50, serving a life sentence for murdering her husband. A short rather rotund, solid woman, she asked me to buy her new girdles. She showed me one of her current items of underwear—a rather tatty high-wasted satin-elastic girdle with hooks and eyes down one side—with four rather large suspenders. Pink. I was detailed to find another exactly like this. A tall order for me not being familiar with such garments. Corsets and girdles were 'out' as far as fashion was concerned. However, advice from one of my officers directed me to a shop just off Seven Sisters Road, a mile or so from the prison.

I found it without too much difficulty—the window was full of the items I was looking for—pink—with bones and laces—all rather dusty and grubby but advertising the very thing. I walked into a tiny Aladdin's Cave, quite dark and musty, but full of amazing garments—amazing to me that is. Two of the walls were lined with old wooden shelves holding long boxes—18 inches to two feet long—for the girdles of course; another wall was lined with draws with see-through glass panels on the front of each draw. Here I glimpsed bras, laces and interlock knickers and other intriguing items. I was startled by a small elderly bespectacled gentleman appearing from behind a curtain. Rather taken aback, I explained what I wanted; he was quite charming and made sure that I bought exactly what was required. I made several visits to this shop and always managed to come back with the right item! The old gentleman was always there and always helpful and courteous.

New clothes were a real treat for so many women and girls. Having lots of new things all at once could be like Christmas.

Sally wrote me a note on a scrappy piece of paper after I had been shopping for her.

Dear Miss Kazumpska

I just want to say thank you for them clothes you bought me yesterday. I never had so many new things before. I always get my sisters old things. Never wot I like. I really like the skirt. I thought you would get me an old ladys one cos I didnt think you listened to me when I said wot I like. But you did. Thank you. Sally.

After she had been discharged, Veronica commented on clothing in a letter to me.

It seemed so strange being pleased and delighted with clothes bought by the prison but I was. Having new things made me feel so much better. They were clean and mine. These new clothes held no memories for me. Miss Bradshaw was so kind when she asked me what kind of things I wanted and she took real trouble getting me the right things. It must have taken her ages. She was very kind.

No one wanted to wear their own clothes for messy jobs — the garden and cleaning party women always wore dungarees. These were brown/khaki coloured bib and brace overalls. Women do not appear to conform well to institutions and will always look for opportunities to be different and express their own personalities. How many different ways can a bib and brace overall be worn? Bib up, bib down, tucked in or hanging out. Legs rolled up, legs rolled down. One leg up and one leg down. Blouse over the top, blouse underneath. Braces tied round the middle, braces hanging down, braces tucked in. Trying to get women and girls to wear a bib and brace in the normal fashion was like pushing water uphill. It couldn't be done. Fine for two minutes but as soon as the wearer felt unobserved back came her personal style. I didn't think it was worth getting upset about. Some of my colleagues liked working parties looking 'smart and tidy' but for me it wasn't worth the hassle for the officers concerned.

Everyone was expected to work during the day and there was a wide variety of work available some of which I described earlier. Cooking in the kitchens, laundry work, working for staff as orderlies or 'red bands', cleaning parties, farms and gardens, library and reception — each institution had a myriad of jobs that needed to be done. There was always a plentiful supply of labour but ... not always of the quality or displaying the commitment staff would have liked! Bullwood Hall and Holloway in particular had factories which offered work for a large number of women and girls (such as the The Holloway Jam factory mentioned in *Chapter 2*, well-known throughout the Prison Service: jam for every prison was made here but this closed before I arrived at Holloway).

The Prison Department had a Prison Industries section which was run on a commercial basis, publishing its trading results every year in the Prison Department Report. Prison Industries and Supplies would fulfil contracts obtained from outside industry as well as making articles for the Prison Department itself. Bullwood specialised in assembly work and machining; Holloway also had a machine workroom, a factory which assembled goods and a tapestry room. The machine rooms made garments for the prison department as well as outside contractors. Clothing for male prisoners accounted for much of the work but there were other contracts for underwear and blouses. Women had the opportunity to learn to be good machinists if they wanted to. However, the majority of women worked on the unskilled assembly lines in the main workrooms.

The factories were staffed by civilian instructors — both male and female. Those I knew were committed and long suffering. It was not an easy task. Most of the work was repetitive and boring. The factory was supervised by both instructors and officers but eyes could not be everywhere.

During my time on the landings as an officer, the Bullwood factory had a contract to assemble men's grooming kits — hairbrush, comb and so on. They were called 'Cavalry sets' if I remember correctly — and were destined for Woolworths, now no longer with us. The borstal girls had to make up the boxes into which the items fitted — these came flat packed, then they put in the comb and brush on an insert and sealed the box. The assembled boxed sets were collected and packed in larger cardboard boxes ready for shipment to the customer. We had an assembly line of sorts. Enthusiastic officers like me exhorted the girls to work hard and we assembled alongside them. Lots of pop music, good humour most of the time and the hours passed.

Some girls made up the boxes, others put in the combs, some the brushes, others sealed the boxes and took them to the packing area. And — one or two bright sparks wrote rude and graphic messages on the back of the inner packaging. An eagle-eyed officer just happened to check one or two boxes and spotted these literary additions. All the last week's work had to be unpacked and checked — several thousand boxes. We never found out if any 'autographed' sets found their way to the customers.

The task changed frequently. Assembling vacuum flasks: putting the fragile glass container into its metal protective casing.

Surreptitiously, take a delicate flask from the box and then, from behind your back, flick it into the air. It is light and goes a long way — it lands with a minor explosion. Can two of us do this at the same time? 'Poof — poof' — shattered gossamer glass fragments everywhere. Innocent faces. Everyone gets the jitters — nobody sees 'who done it'. The officers increase their patrols up and down the lines and the morning passes. It has been fun for some and eventful for others — including me......

For many, the factories and workrooms were excruciatingly boring.

> You think we haven't got brains this — ******* awful mind-numbing stuff that passes for work in this **** place.

Others made the best of it; good work was done; contracts were fulfilled. The sewing rooms made a range of garments and some women learnt a good trade.

Other women practised the skills they had gained outside. Fiona was a hairdresser. Writing from Holloway…

> The hairdressing is still going and we have increased the driers from two to three. New sockets, table with two way mirror and we hope to finally get it extended to the whole prison. When this happens, I shall be so busy I won't have time to think about the next fourteen months.

And a couple of weeks later…

The hairdressing is doing very well and I am thinking of making a takeover bid and buying them out. Only problem — the price — feel it would be a little bit too high!

The women were paid for their work. Jobs had different pay scales. Kitchen work was well-paid in prison terms — normally hard work and long hours in the big prisons like Holloway. Workrooms and factories less so. Fanny wrote from Askham Grange:

You ask for my news — what news?!! What can I say about this place without sounding utterly hypercritical? Let's start on the positive side. Have been allowed to the kitchen working party working on a shift system which gives me a free day after 13.30 every third day. Time does appear to fly working like this. One does not think in terms of seven day weeks but three day ones! And of course the pay is good — the terrific sum of forty eight and half pence [3] and this after only four weeks seems as if the sky is the limit!!! Sit next to Jane in the dining room and one of my roommates is Judy Freeman with whom I understand you are acquainted. Poor old Nelly Jones works in the gardens. She is extremely worried about muscles developing and her complexion becoming rosy. It would appear that the place is not geared to cater for either the working hours or the leisure hours of ninety odd women. For example — I was told to scrub the chopping block — but only the top. Another girl did the sides and yet another did the legs. We were told not to finish for at least three quarters of an hour as this would keep us employed until time for mid-morning break! The blocks by the way are half the area of your office desk. Oh Miss 'K' I just don't know what to do to get myself adjusted here. I've been put back in full medication and this makes me pretty depressed that is should be considered necessary.

A few months later Fanny wrote again mentioning work...

Life here goes on very much a usual. At the last change of work I ended up in the workroom putting sleeves in dolls dresses. At Holloway we could not get a change of work — here we don't want a change but get it every three months.

Not all of the work available was of a mundane nature. In the 1960s Lady

3. Per week. This was 1973.

Anne Tree, daughter of the 10th Duke of Devonshire became a prison visitor having been introduced to the Governor of Holloway by Diana Mosley, her brother's wife's sister. Diana Mosley was married to Sir Oswald Mosley, founder of the British Union of Fascists. Mosley had been imprisoned in Holloway in 1940 under the Defence Regulations and later recommended Lady Anne to the Governor, Miss Davies, as a prison visitor. In an interview in the *Independent* in 2009, Lady Anne said: 'I don't know how people serve long sentences, ... the gloom, the lack of decision for yourself. I was terribly anxious that people should have something to do that was creative...' She set about finding something creative for the women to do — tapestry — which eventually resulted in today's charity, Fine Cell Work which offers prisoners, both men and women, the opportunity to learn a skill and earn a little money for their release by working a range of items from cushion covers to wall-hangings. Lady Ann Tree felt that tapestry might fulfil a positive role in prison, keeping prisoners minds active and creative. In the late-1960s, she persuaded the government and the Governor to set up a tapestry room in Holloway which is where the charity has its roots. Here two women worked quietly in a room in the central administration part of the old prison, not far from the Governor's office.

In the early 1970s, under the beady eye and guidance of a skilled needlewoman, Myra Hindley and Carol Hanson, both sentenced for capital crime, completed a magnificent carpet which had been commissioned by a well-known American politician through the good offices of Lady Ann Tree and her contacts. I understand that many a British politician and dignitary has walked upon this carpet unknowing of its origins! The duty governor of the day was required to visit all parts of the prison every day and dropping into this workroom was a real joy, the work exquisite, the atmosphere calm and creative. I am the proud possessor of a tapestry bookmark and book jacket, both given to me for my birthday. The motif on the book jacket, designed and worked by Myra is of one of Holloway's griffins rampant. Or is it?

How is my dragon? I hope the colours aren't fading, because dragons are magical creatures (your one is a nice type of dragon, not one of the wicked ones, like the one that is in the Hobbit) and never grows old. So I hope he is as bright and as young as ever.

Extract from a letter from Myra 1974

Carol's bookmark says, 'Apart in body but not in mind'. They had saved up and bought the wool and materials from their earnings and made these for me. Sadly the tapestry room was closed some years later but came back in a new format after substantial lobbying of the government by Lady Ann Tree many years later. This new format enabled more women to take advantage of the opportunity.

Everyday life on the wing followed a routine. Women were woken at 6.30, slopped out, tidied their rooms, had breakfast and went to work. Back for lunch on the wing, some association, i.e. free time, then back to work for the afternoon. Women could 'book for the AG' if they had specific requests. Permission to have things sent in, sent out, special visits etc. If the issue was outside an assistant governor's jurisdiction then they booked for the Governor. Booking for the Governor or an assistant governor was a formal event. Women had to book in good time and when booking for the AG they would come down to the wing office after breakfast and wait to be escorted in. I sat behind my desk with the appropriate record book in front of me. The senior officer brought the woman in to stand in front of me — she made her case, I made my decision, recorded it and the woman was escorted out.

Assistant governors also dealt with minor misdemeanours although any which could result in loss of time or substantial loss of privileges were dealt with by the deputy governor or the Governor. It was a little like a court situation. The officer putting the girl 'on report' had to write out the offence against prison rules together with her evidence. A charge sheet was then written up. Any witnesses were also required to write statements which were read out. The big difference was that I was judge and jury. As deputy governor at Bullwood I had quite considerable powers — where warranted; I could delay a girl's release or take away her free association periods for up to 14 days for example. Taking away association meant a girl was kept locked in her room and denied opportunities to spend time out on the wing. Reports were done on the wings or in the Punishment Unit if the inmate in question had had to be taken off the wing because she was violent, aggressive or in any way uncontrollable; or if she needed to be removed from a difficult situation — which may or may not have been of her making. These reports were formal; a woman 'on report' was marched in front of the Governor by two officers — one on either side. Their job was to control the woman and prevent her from attacking the adjudicating officer. On one occasion the officers weren't quick enough and the girl in question was very angry. She managed to tip my desk on top of me, effectively.

Women were paid for the work they did; they could spend this in the prison canteen. Almost all inmates smoked and tobacco was the number one item on almost everyone's canteen list. The women could buy tobacco for rolling or individual cigarettes; the former was more popular. It went further. Collecting the officers' dog ends was the other source of tobacco. In those days most of the officers smoked! Dog ends were guarded but many a blind-eye was turned.

Different work attracted different pay scales. Often the hardest job attracted the highest pay. Kitchen work was highly paid and indeed well-earned. Maximum earnings were in the region of 90 pence — average around 45 pence (decimal coinage was introduced during February 1971). As well as buying the normal toiletries, sweets cigarettes and tobacco, the women could order goods not held in the canteen. This was particularly so for the long-term inmates (LTIs). They were allowed to order foodstuffs and other such items if the officers were prepared to shop for them. Women on D Wing would often save for birthday parties to which they would invite their friends and indeed staff. Parties were normally held at weekends when association periods were much longer — women didn't work at weekends unless they were red bands. D Wing was an open wing which meant that the women were not locked in at all during the day unless there was a real reason for this. Parties were held and enjoyed and I was invited to most. I always popped in but didn't stay too long — not wishing to cramp anyone's style or indeed eat all their hard earned food!

But arrangements didn't always go according to plan…

I still haven't got over my 'thing' about Julie. And I doubt that I ever will. She just bores me more and more, and she's really annoyed Francis and I because we save half our canteen each week so that we can buy coffee and fruit, etc, from a cheaper source outside, and May Smith has been shopping for us. Now its all been stopped — no more teachers can shop and Miss Jenkins decides who will do it, and all because Julie messed it all up by causing problems etc with her shopping which May was doing. Julie over does everything and made sure she was well stocked up before she got the whole thing stopped. I know I sound childish and uncharitable, but she really is a pain in the neck.

Both Holloway and Bullwood Hall had good Education Departments staffed by dedicated and talented teachers. They worked under great pressure and constraint. Discipline staff—prison and borstal officers—and education staff had differing interests and priorities when it came to the women. The former were concerned with security and safety while the education staff focused on learning. Both 'sides' tolerated each other but on the whole they didn't really see eye to eye on many issues. Everyone rubbed along as best they could most of the time but under the surface frustration simmered. The discipline staff found it difficult to understand how the education staff could be as lax as they often were; losing scissors, mislaying keys to cupboards, failing to supervise the use of materials properly, lacking any real commitment to security. The education staff could be really upset when the discipline staff seemed to resent the classes and undermine their work; when their classes were cancelled because there were staff shortages. Education was the first thing to be closed down. Both sides had a point of course and as an assistant governor I trod a narrow path between these conflicting interests. The education departments provided a lifeline for many women and achieved amazing results with often disadvantaged people.

Lorna was an American, serving a long sentence for possession of drugs. She was well-educated, talented and articulate. She wrote to me from Holloway:

Art class is most interesting. Still four of us in it. Sue has three extra classes a week now —for which we're all delighted...because she really has talent...and will certainly do her 'O' level in Art in the near future! Lorain, on the other hand, will only be with us for two more Tuesdays...her release date being on the 19th September (That'll be painful) This weekend, she intends finishing up all her crochet projects...and painting the windows in the stereo room —for which we have permission.

Daily at mid-day I've been doing a hard ¾hour on 'real' English drill with Barbro—a book sent in that is just excellent for English as a second language.

The prison fixed us up with a new TV aerial (no, not for BBC 2 yet), valve, mains plug! And when the workmen were here to fix things up—they moved the set around the room until they found the best spot of reception, which is different to what you recall the location as. And marvellously, in this new spot, the glare off the windows is negligible—hence the art work of Barbro and Jane doesn't have to be covered up with curtains and blinds.

Stores gave us four more mattresses. Dying begins in art class. So soon our stereo room will have lovely rich brown covers- and vivid cushions!

Listen—Miss Neville just opened the door and told me that they had 51 into Reception last night!!! (I was working down there in the late afternoon for an hour) Apparently they all finished work at 2am! A record.

A month later she wrote ranging over the activities of her day:

This is a diary letter!:

Now it is a beautiful, sunny morning…Saturday the 11th…with hopes of exercising-sunbathing in the late morning! Had you heard that our week-day half-three/quarter hour (exercise period) is from 8.30ish to 9.15?? Certainly makes August-September a little annoying! And after that it'll likely be too cool and dark in the morning.

Tonight many of us are going to OT as the guests of the Drug Unit who are putting on two of their own plays…under Judy's[4] direction

You asked about the stereo room. It's used nightly—and usually by a couple of different groups. But the classical records remain untouched except by those of us who like private—room listening in the later hours, the room is kept clean…and someone has it for a weekend job, as well. This past two weeks I had all the records in my cell since Fay was loss of privileges—and I took that opportunity to put the records in order (as Fay asked) and type up three copies of 'numbered stock'. One set of three sheets hangs in the stereo room, another on the board, and Fay keeps the third. So you could say that we are 'advertising our various records.

There are some 69 Beat-and-pop LPs, and some 30 good singles. The classical section is in the 50s; and there are a couple of other smaller divisions. (mind you, in spite of pleas, some of those old junky records keep straying under the £8 needle.)

4.   Education officer.

The wing library is properly underway again. You know who (now on tapestry in her room) has just made cards for another supply of good and different books brought in by one of the teachers.

And on the Holloway front — my job is quite interesting, and its busyness is presently just right. For a while, it was overdone. I primarily work for the Education Department — as their Red Band. Right now, a morning class of girls from either half of the old Remand Centre study from 10 until mid-day. This programme includes a sixth class — Biology — on Monday evenings. The 'deal' is being set up as a 10 week programme ... with each week having one particular theme which all classes adhere to. The English for Foreigners class is getting BIGGER and permission has been granted for we women to assist-teach. (that's on Wed. and Thurs. afternoons) and then I round up the French class for Thursday evening.

Typing assignments come in as always ... there's a big one to do before my home leave. As well as another project. As well as finishing the Education Dept's Library.

One might be forgiven for thinking that I was running a girl's boarding school rather than a prison wing. The Policy for Women and Girls, 1970 set out the aims and purpose of prison for women and the Standing Orders governing the conduct of officers at the time is also clear. The latter quotes the Gladstone Committee of 1895 'to send them out of prison better men and women than when they came in'. Deprivation of liberty *is* the punishment — no one is sent to prison *for* punishment in this country. Boarding schools are or should be about care and the nurturing of the individual and their development. My experience of boarding school had been positive. Without even being aware of it, looking back, I was trying to recreate the same kind of positive experience for the women and girls in my care. I encouraged the girls on borstal recall and the women on D Wing to produce wing magazines; we had poetry readings — inviting well-known poets such as Robert Speight to come and read to us; we had a choir and put on a carol service at Christmas. We had sales of work. The women saved up and hired in films. They came up with lots of different ideas. I tried to ensure that something was always in the offing — something to look forward to.

The Wing Events page in the D Wing magazine describes life on D Wing at a point in time from the particular perspective of those who threw themselves into wing activities:

Since the last issue of 'Behind the Times', we've achieved a number of things community wise, and had several parties, etc, the first of which was on Bonfire Night. As usual we all contributed a few pence form earnings to help pay for the baked potatoes and butter, hot soup and coleslaw which we all very much enjoyed. We played a few records and spent the rest of the evening singing…the only thing missing was the bonfire.

Christmas—a difficult time for many—saw us with a large tree, decorated wing, presents by our door on Christmas morn, and three days of feasting. Spirits were livened up with such games as Bingo and musical chairs. Lots of prizes from the grab-bag! New Years' Eve was celebrated with a variety show, games, hot dogs and chocolates.

The choir mentioned in the first issue was duly enlarged and after a lot of hard work resulted in a memorable performance on28th December. Called a 'Christmas Anthology of Song and Verse', the presentation as a blend of the religious and secular. Readings varied from 'The Burning Babe' by Robert Southwell to an extract from Dickens ' A Christmas Carol.' (We even included a piece by a colonial writer!) As well as the congregation joining in with the familiar carols, the choir sang Percy Buck's 'A Christmas Legend'; 'Thou Must Leave Thy Lowly Dwelling' (music by Berlioz); and the 'Coventry Carol'—all in true Kings College, Cambridge, style!

The silence in the chapel throughout the performance—sadly lacking on other occasions—was to us the surest indication of success, although this was not the only indication. From two of the letters received form visitors with friendly connections with Holloway, we quote the following:

Dear Miss Kozubska

My very grateful thanks to you and all the girls for the wonderful Carol concert you gave us. I don't know when I have enjoyed hearing an evening of singing and readings as much as I did last Thursday. It was certainly worth all the hard work and rehearsing time which must have gone on in the back ground.

Sincerely Yours,
Cameron Visitor

Dear Miss Kozubska

Congratulations on the splendid performance yesterday evening. It really was wonderfully good and you could see they enjoyed doing it and took trouble over it. We were very grateful indeed that we were able to ne there and join in. it was an incredibly good performance by all standards, and most moving. All the more so in the special circumstances.

Friends of Holloway

The Easter/Spring Choir is presently being formed with Back Chorales, spring songs, and a Madrigal to be part of the programme.

Due to Christmas activities, the workshop with its theme of Love, scheduled for December, did not take place but is anticipated in mid-February when we hope to begin highlighting these evenings with outside speakers.

Through the efforts of two women on the wing, A drama Group was started and a play 'Billy Liar' is now being rehearsed—production of which is planned 'sometime'. Perhaps outsiders could come in on an individual basis to offer suggestions or do some readings.

A Welcoming Committee has been formed, comprised of five people whose aim is to make adjusting to the Wing easier for newcomers. As soon as possible after their arrival, a meeting is held for them by members of the committee when the general routine of the wing is explained. Each person on this committee has a specific function—from as concrete a thing as supplying cell kit....to creating an interest in optional wing activities. The Netball Team recently played their first match (or should we say 'battering'!) against members of the Drug Unit, and won by 10 to 4. They certainly had us worried, though, especially when they won the first two goals in as many minutes, with probably half their Staff, including their AG, and the rest of their women cheering them on. We certainly felt their community spirit! At half time the other side revived us with wedges of orange and lemon, and at the end of the match treated us to a packet of cigarettes. Already we are anticipating our next match! (unfortunately they are now practicing daily A table tennis tournament is already being planned with this same unit, and this time we will do the entertaining.

You can see that we have increased our community events!

Ground floor of F Wing or Borstal Recall sometimes called FDX

(see page 29)

CHAPTER 7

............................Day

I woke that Friday morning looking forward to my four days away starting at 5 pm that evening—we worked ten days on, four days off in those days. I went to bed that night in a real turmoil. Seeing my borstal recall girls on the roof of Holloway Prison on BBC TV news, throwing shoes at the Governor did nothing for my peace of mind.

I woke up one Tuesday morning knowing I had a couple of case conferences and a magistrates' visit. One Saturday I went to bed late having spent several hours talking to a young woman determined to cut her wrists. One Wednesday I had a shopping trip. One Thursday I went to East Sutton Park for a meeting. Every day was different for me. I had no idea what it had in store for me. I was never bored.

But the women's days could be long and boring, never ending. Sometimes days could be full of despair, at other times full of hope. Would the Parole Board grant parole? For some, too much time to think; or was it lots of time to plan for the future? For others, time to liven things up on the wing.

Bethan Grey was in her late 30s. Sentenced to six years for fraud and theft, I first met her on D Wing at Holloway early in 1972. This wasn't her first sentence either. We got on well although I don't remember us having anything particular in common. We had good chats and I got to know her reasonably well. Her previous sentences had been a trial for her and indeed for the prison. She could be stroppy and difficult—going out of her way to cause trouble. Bethan had no convictions for serious violence and she was reasonably behaved with me on D Wing, both of which made her a candidate for open prison. Against a considerable amount of opposition, I recommended that she be transferred to Askham Grange open prison in Yorkshire. Over the next six months she wrote to me regularly and, judging by her letters, I must have written to her regularly.

2nd August

Dear Miss K

Just a few lines to thank you very much for giving me the opportunity to come here, it really is super, and full of surprises, it's certainly going to make this sentence a whole lot easier.

I have palled up with a friend of Martha's, who is a real nice girl and she is showing me the ropes gradually. I honestly think that anyone who refuses the chance to do their sentence here is a fool to themselves.

The other purpose of this letter is to ask you if you could please look into what happened to my fur coat. I put it into the office to be returned to property when I was on D Wing, and when I left, I figured it had probably been put in my case, but when I arrived here it was not in my property. I'd be ever so grateful if you could arrange to have it sent to me with the next escort coming here.

I have not yet asked Miss Morgan about sending you some material for the D Wing paper, but I have not forgotten and will get round to it in a day or two. When Miss Morgan saw me she asked what I had done to deserve to be here. I had to smile, but I intend to prove to her that I have changed since she knew me, just as I did to the Holloway Officers. If it's OK with you, and permitted here, I'll drop you a line occasionally and let you know how I am doing, as you really did more than your share to help me find my feet in this sentence.

Give my regards to Miss Fortune and thank her for being a super escort here, congratulate Miss Fox on her engagement for me and please say Hello to Sister Wedge and all my friends on D Wing, especially Sue, who I still miss a great deal, even with all the amenities provided for my recreation over here.

Must rush, it's time for work.

With all good wishes—sincerely Bethan

19th August

Dear Miss K

Many thanks for your kind letter received the other day and for the coat I got a few days before, brought up by Mrs Little. Yes, I was still on D Wing when you planned the 'Folk Evening'. I do hope it is a success, because knowing you, you have put a great deal of effort into it. It was also good to read the response you are getting for the wing magazine. I guess any literary effort I may produce are to be used for the magazine 'Open Door' which they are hoping to start publishing again here, it appears that it died a natural death some while ago and the Assistant Governor is trying to resurrect it.

I was very pleased to see Betty arrive here, as she was able to give me all the news of D Wing because I really do miss the girls there especially Sue. The women here are not quite as friendly as the D Wing girls. Perhaps I haven't been here long enough. They have all the same dramatics here as they do in Holloway and which I once used to be a part of, but fortunately here you can get away from it and take a stroll in the gardens. I wouldn't want Miss Morgan's job for all the tea in China.

I have now been moved out of the workroom, on to the gardens and it's really great, particularly as the weather has been pretty good. You'd be really proud of me, as I am ambassador of your good judgement if you saw me in my bib overalls about three sizes too big, enormous wellington boots, that take all my strength to lift one before the other, rubber gloves, and a pick axe over my shoulder. At present I'm digging a trench to plant a hedge around Miss Morgan's house. I feel like an Amazon, or a member of the chain gang, sentenced to hard labour, but seriously, it's a lot of fun, even if it is darn hard work.

My morning job here is to vacuum and dust the centre before 7.15am and at that time I'm not even fully conscious. And some of the officers tease me and say it's the most privileged job in the place. My retort is that Miss Austin who is Chief here and was once my PO, is getting back at me for being such a fiend when she knew me! Every morning without fail, there is a dead fly on the window ledge, which I swear blind she puts there deliberately to see if I do my job properly. But I haven't blotted my copy book yet, as I'm determined not to let you down or myself for that matter. I gather you will probably be paying a visit to Askham Grange sometime in October. I do hope you won't pass through without seeing me. I'd love to see you again—mind you you'll have to look extra hard to find me in the foliage if I am still on the gardens.

I am hoping I am not forgotten here for my birthday next month and that someone remembers to send me a birthday card at least. We have just had an election here to vote in a house committee, another project that has been in operation before, but appears to have faded out too. I hope it has a longer life this time and is instrumental in bringing about the reforms that are required. The staff are pretty co-operative and certainly very approachable.

Yesterday I was interviewed by Miss Brown about the hostel scheme so I guess I'll be before the September selection board, but as Miss Brown said, not everyone gets this opportunity. So all I can do is keep my fingers crossed and wait patiently.

I enjoy writing to you as I can say anything that's on my mind, and because of your position I don't have to think around everything. It's Sunday afternoon and visits have just started. Betty tried to haul me outside, but unlike her, I am quite accustomed to being free to roam and I've chosen to catch up on my sleep in preparation for another week of digging trenches. Well, bye for now, please write when you can.

Sincerely Bethan

27 August

Dear Miss K

Thanks a million for your letter received just a short while ago. Thought I'd answer it during my lunch hour right away — Tuesday afternoon — before Mr Wellgood, my boss, completely kills me off in those darned gardens.

I've got Betty with me on them as of yesterday. She's had me in fits, she spent the best part of half an hour filling up a wheelbarrow with rocks that had to be moved from point A to B, got it so full that when she went to wheel it the whole thing tipped over and she had to start from scratch, muttering curses under her breath. She's got boots and overalls even bigger than mine, so we really are a fine representation of D Wing.

Before I go any further, you really have let the side down. We always looked to you as a pal rather than an AG and now your latest <u>AMBASSADOR</u> from D Wing to here, has really shown your true colours! Whatever did we do to deserve her? She's causing havoc here, claiming that those of us who knew her on D wing have been threatening her, and as God is my witness, none of the three of us have said a single word to her, not 'hello' 'kiss my foot' or anything.

Both Liz and Betty asked to be remembered to you. And Liz said she hates saying goodbye, and after you'd been so good to her, she would have been upset if she had had to see you before she left, so it was for the best that she didn't. She likes it very much here, and feels sure that Paula Strong will too. I think most anybody would prefer it to Holloway.

We had a party here for the bank holiday too. And a dance in the ballroom which the majority of the staff attended. A buffet supper was laid on and it was quite a gas. We even had a man to dance with, one of the officer's husband. He was quite a dish too, but a prison officer!!!

I do hope your folk evening and the holiday shindig were a success. I'd have given my eye teeth to see you as Mary Poppins and Ronnie Corbett or was it Mary Hopkins and Ronnie Barker? I understand Miss Phillips was taking part in this enterprise too, it all happens after I've left, not at all fair of you.

As Betty told you in her letter, we are both founder members of a dramatic society along with two other girls—we have started practising a one act play called 'Right of way'. It's a comedy about a woman who buys a house that has been built in the middle of a public right of way, and the locals have suddenly decide to exercise their legal right—and stroll right through the middle of the house. I'm playing the part of an old deaf lady who thinks that even the bus goes through the house—it's a lot of fun doing it, and I'm sure when we put it on for the girls in about a month, they should get as much enjoyment out of it as the participants.

I've just been reading your letter—that southern fried chicken sounded 'finger licking good' and I could just visualize you shopping for six chickens. Bet the 'normal shoppers' (quote) thought 'She's young to have such a big family'. Did it divide OK?

Tell Sue not to worry about her new job, she'll still get the 'dog ends'. That's more than I do and I have to be up at 6.30 to clean the centre before breakfast, only to find that they've been burnt as per instructions from higher up. Never mind, July's only ten months away. I've even been done out of my birthday present from Sue, the fraud! But I'll still be looking forward to a card from you anyway. How about that for cheek?!!

Love to everyone—sincerely from all three of us—Bethan

30 September

Dear Miss K

Many thanks for your letter received the other day. It was really nice to know that you thought to write even from home. I had to smile when I received the letter, as the censoring officer had written right across the envelope 'From J Kozubska'. You must have had her a bit confused as you signed off with just a flourishing monogram of 'JK'. You had of course put the prison address at the head of your letter, I guess that was the vital clue to the mystery of who 'JK' from Bourne-mouth — Poole was, as that was the stamp on the envelope. Anyway — all's well that ends well, I got the letter and that was the main thing.

Thanks for the birthday wishes. It was on the 12th of the month and I did have a nice day as could be expected under the circumstances. Betty, together with a few other friends saw to that but I did miss Sue.

The dramatics were very short lived, unfortunately they met with too much in surmountable opposition from the powers that be. They have been replaced by dramatics of a less favourable type, the star role being played by Mary — she has been instrumental in getting me my very first report of this sentence, but fortunately I only lost 14 days pay and not my very valuable remission — as did another girl who was involved with her. I saw Miss Morgan in a private interview and told her all about the havoc she created on D Wing, and Miss Morgan said just to stay away from her as she was aware of what she was like, but as you know, she thrives on such incidents and causes trouble at every possible opportunity. No doubt in time she will get her just desserts.

Today (date of issue of this letter) the new change of work has gone up, as of Monday I am no longer on the gardens. I start the Punch Card Course, which I was so hoping to get. Towards the end of my reign on the gardens, my job took on an added interest in the form of eight baby ducklings, hatched just over a fortnight ago. I was put in sole charge of feeding them and all the other ducks (twenty nine of ours and about a dozen wild mallard) and cleaning out the duck house. The babies are delightful, they go swimming now, and look like a miniature Henley Regatta. I'm rather sorry to leave them.

Keep your fingers crossed for me to be successful on the course, because if I am, I will probably get a job directly. The course finishes on 22 December and I will be able to go on to the hostel, for my last six months.

Well—must close for now, usual stationary problem, don't forget to send me a copy of the first D Wing Magazine if that's permissible.

Best wishes—sincerely Bethan

30 October

Dear miss K

I thought it about time I wrote to you again and let you know how all the D Wing representation are doing. To begin with myself—I have started the punch card operators' course. In fact I am two weeks under way with it and finding it very interesting. I've had a couple of speed tests. In the alpha section of exercises based on the key board, I did 9,400 odd key depressions per hour, which was top of the class I'm proud to say, with a lead of 4,000 on the other three girls in the class. This was no doubt because I have previous typing experience and even though its been a long while my fingers are still pretty nimble. In the numeric test, run a few days later, I did 7000 odd key depressions. I was ahead in that one too by about 3,000. Figures has never been my strong point so I was pretty pleased at the result. My mind boggles at the mere sight of figures normally.

We were a bit late starting the course as the teacher had been away on vacation to Majorca and contracted some kind of virus, but she still thinks that there is no reason why we should not finish it by the scheduled date, which is the 22nd of December. The instructress is trying to get an examination paper set for us by the London Institute of City and Guilds. If she is successful we will have a certificate to show for our pains, that is of course assuming we pass. So keep your fingers, toes, eyes and everything else crossed for me.

I was up before the hostel board earlier this month, but since I had already been accepted for the course, Miss Morgan said I would be up again in January, and if I am successful, I may be able to get a job as a punch card operator in York.

This will be a great help as I will certainly need the money when I get out of here, and have to start afresh outside.

There is a lot of speculation at the moment about the effect the new Penal Reform Bill will have on those of us who are eligible for parole, but I'm not even indulging in such whims, as I really don't stand to gain a tremendous amount form parole anyway.

We are expecting to see you here one of these days on a visit. Everyone else appears to be on the agenda for paying us a visit. Polly Elwess, the TV personality is coming on Thursday and apparently a rep from Helen Rubenstein, one from Esteé Lauder, and a fashion consultant are all forth coming attractions.

Give my good wishes to everyone leaving D Wing soon and wish luck to all those still there. I am still not sure if I'd rather be there than here, Holloway definitely has its advantages even though that may sound strange with the obvious amenities afforded to us here.

Well, so much for the present, give my regards to all the D Wing staff. Please write when you have time. We all share your letters and look forward to them

Best wishes Bethan

26 November

Dear miss K

Many thanks for your letter received the other day, which I duly passed around for the perusal of all ex-D Wing girls — well nearly all would be more correct!! We are all now eagerly awaiting the advent of the wing magazine and will be most disappointed if it does not arrive — it appears that I have been appointed official letter writer for the group of us. Liz and Betty are both sitting here with bits of gossip they want relayed none of which is at all relevant I assure you!

We only have three complete weeks left on the course and today we had a lecture from a systems analyst from a firm in Leeds. All about computerisation, and data processing. It was most enlightening and he has arranged for us to go and visit the company sometime in the next few weeks, so as to give us an insight into the authentic atmosphere.

Betty has her name down for the next punch card operators course starting in the New Year, she's in charge of the ducks at the moment. Liz is now in the laundry. With my kind of luck, I guess, if I don't get one to the hostel scheme in January I'll probably get the rotten ducks back, and be skating around the frozen duck pond trying to break the ice in spots for the little darlings to swim in.

Its bitter cold here at present and the wind has been blowing at some alarming velocity. I thank heaven for the central heating and don't feel too kindly about having to go on the gardens on Saturday mornings. I come back in a dozen shades of purple and too stiff to move for at least a quarter of an hour. Betty's stamina at braving those winds amazes me no end. She seems blissfully at home in all this arctic weather.

I have had all my parole interviews. I think I told you, so I am now awaiting the results.

Well that's all for now—regards form the 'three of us' Betty, Liz and Bethan.

12 December

Dear Miss K

Just had another couple of arrivals from your way and I got to see Miss Ball who has been a long standing favourite of mine for ages. She gave me all the current news but unfortunately none from D Wing.

I have already finished the computer course. On Friday we are going to Leeds to look round a computer installation. It should be quite interesting and will be a pleasant day out.

Needless to say Polly Elwess was the only one of the visiting dignitaries that materialized. Helena Rubinstein and Estee Lauder reps all went by the board.

A number of the girls were informed today of their new release dates, after the remission time on their remand time had been calculated , and Betty gained six weeks. She is highly elated as you can imagine. No such luck for me. I never was on remand worse luck.

The hostel board is not normally till the first Thursday of the month, so I have quite a wait before I hear if I am fortunate enough to get the hostel. I do hope

I am. It will give me some incentive and I could certainly use the money when I get out as I have to start from scratch. It seems absolutely ages since I was in Holloway but on reflection it's only four and half months. The time here seems to drag terribly. I don't know if all the freedom to roam has anything to do with creating that illusion. I haven't joined any classes here as the course absorbs all my powers of concentration during the day and by the evening comes around I'm so thoroughly exhausted and seeing double. They have rather good classes here though—shorthand, typing, speedwriting, basic English, general studies, cooking, pottery crocheting, needlework and handicraft are some of them.

All the best from Betty, Liz and me!!

Sincerely Bethan

25 February 73

Dear Miss K

Sorry for the tardiness in not replying to your letter, or thanking you for both the issues of 'Behind the Times' received safely. You and my friends on D Wing, of who few probably remain, have not been forgotten. It's just that with only a limited amount of letters to write out, and a lot of friends writing in, it becomes increasingly difficult to fit everyone in.

May I beginning by saying how very much the D Wing publication was enjoyed at Askham. I passed my issue around among the girls, who like myself, were very impressed by both the quality of your magazine and the amazing amount of literary talent it lent scope to. Congratulations, and keep up the good work, and do please continue to send me all the forthcoming issues, as they afford me with at least an evening's entertainment and I frequently re read many articles—I shall be here till the 16th July, and I also plan on keeping in touch with you after that I if may.

I should be able to write you more regularly now, because as of the 1st of March, we are going to be allowed to buy as many canteen letters as we care to, and there is no longer going to be any censoring of mail, either coming in or going out—I'm sure you will agree that this is big step in the right direction—I did hate second hand mail.

The prison grape vine was all agog a few weeks ago with news of a 28 year old Gov to replace Miss Morgan, and I sat with bated breath waiting to hear it was you, and I could hang out the flags , spread the red carpet etc. I did realize that the rumour had exaggerated your age by some twelve months!! But I still hoped till the press rudely shattered all my hopes as they are wont to do...

...my only regret is that it is not going to be you. However if the powers that be permit it, I shall make it a point to buy you lunch in town when I get out, as I'd love to see you again. It's not often I feel an affinity with authority. I've always been classed as distinctly anti-authority, but it will be great to have someone who knows all, and can give much needed advice.

Our pantomime was a roaring success, and netted a nice little nest egg I gather, and we are now in the throes of another sale of work, the second during my stay here. I have made a few items, but my proudest achievement is the soft toy—an elephant—I completed yesterday. Even Miss Morgan says he is fabulous—I rather surprised myself—I made him in the work room, where I am back working after having completed the computer course, with the highest speed in the class. I didn't get the hostel—reason given, being my previous record. A fact that released momentary bitterness, which has since evaporated I'm please to say, and I'm looking forward to July now and freedom.

No other news for now, so I'll close and use remaining paper to submit my contribution to the next issue of your mag—with kind regards and much love to all on D Wing—Bethan.

I have no other letters from Bethan and sadly I do not know how life worked out for her. Although I knew something of her family background and her offences, we never discussed either in our letters.

Bethan's life at Askham Grange was in stark contrast to some of the lives of those who served their sentences at Holloway. Sentences in Holloway for women ranged from a few days, a few months, a couple of years—to life sentences. Young women sentenced to borstal training or recalled to borstal spent from six months to two years at either Bullwood Hall or on DX, the Borstal Recall Wing at Holloway. In the main, my experience was limited to borstal girls and women serving long-term sentences of over three years. The long term inmates tended to have a mature outlook on life. The women on D Wing wanted to live there as quietly as possible; of course they had their ups and downs but it was unusual to see the coarse, aggressive and perhaps more disturbed behaviour often depicted in the media—TV, books and films. It was not in the women's interest to behave badly because this normally resulted in tension on the wing, punishment and/or a loss of time—a delay in their release date. I rarely experienced much of the desperate and difficult behaviour often found in other parts of Holloway. However, I led a much more turbulent life on the Borstal Recall Wing at Holloway and at Bullwood Hall

There was a huge contrast between some of my experiences on borstal recall and on D Wing; the main and most obvious being the behaviour and demeanour of volatile young teenage girls against the maturity of grown women serving long sentences. The girls on the Borstal Recall Wing had huge problems; many of them had serious mental health problems. Almost all of them had difficult relationships with their parents; others had problematic relationships with boyfriends and partners. Many had been unable to control their behaviour in the community—some even choosing to be recalled by breaking the terms of their borstal licence. A recall to borstal tended to indicate an 'extreme' somewhere along the line. There were rarely more than 18 girls on DX, the Borstal Recall Wing. DX was a psychotherapeutic wing—supervised by a consultant psychotherapist but run by an assistant governor and discipline officers. This in itself gave rise to real clashes, obvious even to the girls themselves. Here is the editor of the Borstal Recall Wing magazine, *In and Out* writing about the situation she experienced:

Hi There

This is now the third magazine that FDX community have produced, in my opinion it is the best. Al the time we are trying to improve the standard. Another thing, the printing process is one big hassle as we just don't seem to have a cheap and adequate method in the prison of reproducing it; so if it is not quite unto standard I hope you will understand.

We have recently had many changes on the wing, and quite a few of our girls have left which now brings us down to thirteen. Nevertheless we are still trying to become a community instead of a bundle of Borstal brats; this is much harder to achieve than we thought it would be. It sees strange to think of ourselves as one although it's a good thing, for we learn to care for one another and understand one another's problems We are normally an 'I'm all right Jack' community. We have reached the stage where the staff care for the staff and perhaps care for the girls too, but the girls cannot seem to accept that the staff do care: although for each other you could not find such loyalty anywhere else. At present, the biggest problem is the barrier between the staff and the girls but only time will tell if it will break at all. I do not for a minute blame either staff or girl, but the situation. After all the Recall Centre is smack in the middle of a grossly overcrowded prison; where one cannot bend the rules too much for obvious reasons. Therefore it's difficult to run a therapeutic wing when one has to abide by the rules of the prison. Personally I think one cannot combine therapy and discipline and expect perfect results. Meanwhile we will struggle on and let you know how things go.

I think she had a point but I didn't agree with her view altogether. As for so many, discipline appeared to be a negative issue rather than an integral part of life for our editor.

It was difficult not to be moved by so many personal stories. I found them heart-breaking. Here, another youngster writes about her feelings:

It seems funny in a way to be sitting here writing this. Exactly a year ago tonight I sat in a cell at Bullwood Hall borstal and wrote: 'Tonight is the last time I will ever be 15, tomorrow is my birthday. I wonder where I will be this time next year?' then I got up and stood looking out of the window, thinking how much I loved my boyfriend. Two years ago tonight on the eve of my fifteenth birthday, I stood by the window of a cell in Newport House Remand Home and looked out across the fields thinking of the future. It seems only a few months have passed since then but it's two whole years. Ha! I packed a lot of living into those two years, I spent 14 or 15 months of it in these places.

Tonight is the last time I will ever be 16. I hope and pray that the future will be better. Please God, let me find true happiness soon. I'm really going to try in the future, and will, this time next year be free.

In addition to their main role of imprisonment, all penal establishments were 'total' institutions caring for the women's everyday physical and social needs; they provided shelter, food and warmth, clothing, medical care, education and employment with varying degrees of success for a diverse population of women of all ages, 15-year-old youngsters to old age pensioners. For some, prison and borstal offered a home and companionship—for others, the loss of their liberty alone was a real and excruciating punishment.

A young borstal girl had this to say...

> When I get locked away I feel like my whole worlds has fallen to dust about my feet. I've never really had anyone to care for me, unless of course you call orphanages, children's home and approved schools places of care. To me all they mean is a roof over my head and food in my mouth, and perhaps a small sense of security. I feel society is a little hasty when dealing with people like me. I'm not a criminal, just a young girl searching for an answer. How can I ever hope to find it when all I have ever known in an institution? How can I lead a normal stable life when I don't even know what life outside is really like?

Such activities, wing magazines and choirs invariably had a fall out somewhere along the line! I was naïve but probably no more so than my Governor. She was quite supportive but neither of us envisaged the headlines in *Titbits* which put a damper on our publishing 'empire'. The D Wing magazine editorial panel had decided that they would have a problem page—Betty Busybody's Problem Page. And yes—this gave us a real problem. Who sent the magazine to *Titbits*? We shall never know. Why were *Titbits* interested? Betty Busybody answered questions about everyone's prison love life and of course love life in prison means only one thing.

Cameo 3: A glimpse of a dying woman sentenced to hang for murder

Bertha Mary Scorse stabbed her lover Joyce Dunstan after a row. Together with two members of her family, Mary had gone to see Joyce after an altercation. They took a taxi. When Joyce came out of her house to meet them, Mary stabbed her to death.

Joyce and Mary both suffered from TB. They met when they were patients together at the Tehidy Sanatorium in Cornwall. They had lived together for nearly two years after their discharge.

Mary's TB surfaced again and she was carried in to Exeter Assizes on a stretcher. She was charged with murder and found guilty. Her stretcher was held at an angle as she was sentenced to death by hanging. The death sentence was commuted because she was believed to be dying.

Mary Scorse was small and unattractive; her undoubted powers of seduction were not immediately obvious. For some, she was an archetypal lesbian — normally dressed in a pair of blue jeans and shirt, with short-cropped hair and male shoes. Supporting and helping her was an unenviable task and not for the fainthearted. She could be manipulative and destructive and was frequently a source of turbulence wherever she was. However, she had served her time and was due for release on licence. Mary had been given the opportunity to settle back into the community gradually. Although nominally on the D Wing roll, she went out to work every day. Monitored as a normal employee when at work, yes, but she wasn't supervised during the time she was outside the prison. The point of the exercise was to help her adjust to the outside world after years of institutional living. Mary spent her weekends on the wing with all the other women. She kept a low profile, keen that her release was not jeopardised by any incidents. I had little to do with her; she had a probation officer and was looked after by one of my AG colleagues.

Sometimes officers joined the Prison Service at a very young age. Phillipa Smart was one such officer on D Wing. Still on probation, she had been on D Wing for about six months. Pale, tiny and slight with long dark hair tied back in a ponytail. Fine featured, eager and earnest, her blue uniform almost overwhelmed her. Phillipa came from a very rural community in Northern Ireland; her family were devoted to her and anxious that she do well. She worked hard and had the makings of a successful career ahead of her. But Phillipa was naïve, idealistic and gullible. She was easy prey.

The first I heard of it was one morning, about 8 am when the staff came on. Phillipa had taken an overdose—half-hearted but an overdose. One of her colleagues had found her in the officer's hostel—she had been taken to hospital but was now back in her room. No one was clear about the reason for Phillipa's actions but the word was that Mary Scorse was involved.

Not understanding, I went over to see Phillipa. I found her distraught. Crying uncontrollably. Through the tears and her reticence she told me that her life wasn't worth living. She had been rejected by her lover and she could not see a way forward. There was no purpose to her life anymore. The senior medical officer and the Governor were obviously involved but she would not talk to them. She was my officer, I knew her as well as anyone. Slowly, slowly the story unfolded. Phillipa had got to know Mary when she was on duty at weekends. Mary had suggested that they meet outside the prison during the week—have coffee, go places. Phillipa agreed. They met in secret for several months. Mary had declared undying love for Phillipa and they had made plans together for the time when Mary would finally be released on licence.

The day before, Phillipa saw Mary on the wing with another woman. She confronted Mary who laughed and scoffed at her, rejecting her completely.

Tea and sympathy was not appropriate. Phillipa was suicidal and likely to try to take her life again. I contacted her parents who came immediately. But they were shocked and completely out of their depth. They had no idea how to cope with their own feelings about what had happened although they desperately wanted to support their daughter. Phillipa didn't want them near her—she knew that they couldn't understand.

The SMO found a place for her at a clinic and I took Phillipa there—eventually to start to come to terms with her experience and to rebuild her life.

Mary Scorse was released on licence after 31 years in prison.

CHAPTER 8

Friends and Lovers

Billy was a tall woman, broad in the shoulders and narrow-hipped with dark hair carefully cut into a short-back-and-sides. She wore blue jeans and an open-necked shirt and stood in large, size nine brogues. Under her shirt she wore a girdle to restrict her breasts. How do I know? Because I bought it for her. She was entitled to one under the prisoner's clothing allowance mentioned in *Chapter 6*.

Some people found it difficult to understand what Gabriella saw in Billy. She was as fair as Billy was dark, with long golden tresses tied up in a pony-tail most of the time. Billy and Gabriella were an 'item' as we would say nowadays. They were both serving sentences for theft, two and four years respectively — Billy was due for release well before Gabriella. Theirs was a real prison romance.

I don't know the ins and outs of their relationship but I do know that they were a devoted couple. They shared a cell — a number of cells on D Wing were double cells so this was nothing out of the ordinary and I had no reason under Prison Rules to deny their request to share. There were no overt displays of affection or anything more; nothing that outwardly might upset anyone. But we all knew that they were 'together'. They told us so and were proud of their relationship.

Life doesn't run smoothly for anyone and it was no different for these two. I had a responsibility to transfer women to open prison if their behaviour warranted this. HMP Styal normally had beds and Holloway was always bursting at the seams which meant that I was always looking for women to transfer. It was never popular and women were frequently upset when they were told they had to go. We tried to keep women who lived in the south at Holloway but it wasn't always possible. And it wasn't possible in this case. Gabriella had to go.

8.3.73
Dear Miss Kay

I was reminiscing on the better days of Holloway, and recalled a sad one instead. The day I was upset because Penny was sent to Local [prison]......I knew then that one renounces all right of self government when imprisoned.

Despite all the facts, I hope you have forgiven me for being wayward.

I am writing to you after being out of your jurisdiction for six weeks during which I have searched and found that you were perfectly right about therapy being inside oneself. The groups and lectures were not in vain. Here one needs all the training and self control they can muster to even exist. I am truly glad I learned a few things in Holloway which I can utilize here. The things that are in me..........

I had to laugh the other day when I heard that the girls in Holloway were doing a survey on the canteen prices. Things are far dearer here than in Holloway. E.g 1 Lux soap 7½ compared to 6½, tobacco 19p and so on.

My job in here is a good one. I work outside in the Church. I adore it and am proud of my best workmanship. I get a good wage as well 51p.

Miss Kay, I regret leaving Holloway and D Wing, and especially you, because after ten months in prison I have never met anyone so understanding.....even taking your bad temper into consideration! Don't give up the groups or any of the therapeutic things on D Wing. They certainly allow one to realise their sense of values, especially when they are without.

My regards to all those who deserve them

Yours truly
Gabriella

23.3.73
Dear Miss Kay

I got your letter today and the joy and surprise prompted an instant reply.

I had faith in your replying to my letter, although it was hinted that you may be far too busy to bother. I know the humanitarian side of you could never have flown away since I left Holloway.

About the incident on leaving Holloway, I never dreamt of taking your actions personally. I knew your position and respected it. It was not your fault.

It saddens me to hear about the Spring Choir, because I would give my right arm to be in that. There is a church choir here, which has about ten girls at a time. As you know the church choirs are not so very attractive despite the fact that you get a gown to wear here.

As you know I work alone outside the prison gates in the two beautiful churches. I polish the floors and generally keep everything spic and span. I am very much in love with the churches and they compensate for my discontent here. The peace and quiet gives me every opportunity to check out my mind, to overhaul myself.

There is no news of my parole as yet. The date is 10.5.73. Hope to get it so we can have that coffee. The family are fine. they visited me last weekend. The first visit due and taken. I was especially thrilled to read about Billy. I hope things there are the same with her. Nothing has changed, but improved in my mind. She leaves on Monday. Try to convey my 'everything' to her.

Your letter is the best thing that happened to me since I got here. The words 'battle on' have helped to materialise the once foggy future here. I will try to live up to the teachings of D Wing. They were strong sound basic essential to good living...I am glad of my experience on D Wing.

Have the 'wedding bells' chimed for Miss Smith and Miss Houseman?

Love to all and write soon

Yours truly

Gabriella

30. 6. 73

My Dear Miss K,

Billy and I got your lovely letter and we were both happy to hear from you.

I got parole and Billy was there to collect me and take me home.

...May be if it hadn't been for you we wouldn't know what living is all about and return to our old routine. You really deserve a medal for humanity.

I imagine your boys are the happiest in the world, simply because they have you. I don't blame them for whistling. By the way, my family isn't too bad with Billy as on her release she came straight to them and spilt the beans. She has been with the family since then. They mourn but it gets lesser and lesser every day. We are quite happy together and hope to see you when you come to London.

By the way Billy and I are thinking if going into business.

We are yours truly
Billy and Gabriella

23. 10. 73
Our very own Miss K

After seeing the Harvest festival Service on television, Billy and I decided that although you have not answered our last letter we should forgive you, as you may be very busy training your boys for a better future, like you always did with us.

As you may observe for the address above, we have now got a flat of our own, and we are doing fine. We don't own a business as yet but we hope to very soon......

I must give you some wing gossip. Lucy Moth my roommate has been re arrested for firearms and is on bail. Dotty is a sort of West End Bum (They are not together). Hannah is OK so is Babs Brown. Miss Mini has a new home and made a huge mistake by taking in Jill Day, who turned her over, and who during her stay at Miss Mini's was a constant alcoholic, and pure trouble.

We have seen quite a few of the girls but have kept far away because in our house there is no room for hangers on. You'll agree won't you?

Now down to Billy and I. We are doing OK, and we have got the children. She is a very good partner, except she drinks. I found a way to help her stay sober. I have given her my car and as soon as she gets her licence back I am sure she will stay sober.

You won't be surprised to know that I have put on weight because I now eat with Bill and the kids! As you know I never used to eat a thing.

Miss K, I hope my letter is not too boring, as I would love to hear from you as soon as possible, because we are extremely grateful for every effort you put in making us as good as we really are.

We are your protégés
Billy and Gabriella

As was often the case I do not have any other letters from Gabriella and I don't know how the story ended. Did she and Billy make it? I don't know but I hope so. They were a devoted couple trying to make a go of it together. Billy came from a really unstable background and her sexual orientation made life difficult for her. Her parents weren't interested, in fact they were horrified at the way she lived and chose to dress. Such a reaction was more often than not the norm 40 years ago. Gabriella's family were staunch church-goers — very evangelical. How Gabriella squared her lifestyle with her religion I don't know. I had the impression that her preferences weren't in line with church teaching. However, her family were magnificent and accepted this odd couple which was the better illustration of love and faith in my book.

Did I write back — I hope so. I tried to respond until the writer didn't need to write anymore but I am sure sometimes didn't keep it up. Looking back, I have absolutely no idea how I managed to write what must have been so many letters.

Gabriella and Billy were unusual in that they had a relationship that was intended to continue on release. Most relationships were a response to the situation in which women and girls found themselves. For many people, it isn't easy to live without love, affection and sex whether this be within a penal establishment, a prisoner-of-war camp, a boarding school, the armed forces or any other 'total' institution. People make the best of situations and so did the women.

The Friendship

We have known each other for just three weeks,
My heart is breaking, my body so weak,
You brought happiness to my life,
When all I had was pain and strife.

The time has come when we must part,

And when you leave you'll break my heart.

I want to die, I feel so lonely,

To me you are my one and only.

You showed me the path to ecstasy,

Forever your memories will live inside me.

My mind will always remember,

The love we once shared in the month of November.

God bless you and keep you in struggles and strife.

I will love my darling for the rest of my life.

Poem published in the D Wing Magazine.

This poem will scan—almost—with a little effort! It isn't difficult to understand the writer's feelings. She wrote it after a brief relationship—the writer arrived on the wing just a few weeks before her newly found lover was discharged.

When I joined the Prison Service in 1971, I had little understanding of same sex relationships and no real feeling about them either way. At Bullwood Hall, as a temporary officer before going to Wakefield for my assistant governor training, I learned about lesbianism in a gentle way. It existed within the borstal in both the staff and girls' communities. It wasn't particularly overt—these relationships could be found in both cultures and we all got to know about them. It certainly wasn't rife. No one was judgemental. This is how things were for a small minority of staff and girls. Lesbianism wasn't an offence against prison discipline. Homosexuality had been decriminalised in the UK in 1967, and female homosexuality had never been a criminal offence. If things did get out of hand and problems occurred, girls were reported for the outcomes—more often than not fighting over some perceived slight or indeed a rival suitor—not sexual orientation.

The most overt shows of anything sexual occurred when the girls were listening to music and dancing. Some would dance in the most provocative of ways, often entwined together with knees strategically placed. The officers intervened if things became too obvious. Occasionally if they wanted to shock, girls would kiss passionately but this was rare and prompted officers to put a stop to the display immediately. I don't believe that many girls were confirmed lesbians—most met each other's needs at a specific time in their lives. When released I guess they normally returned to their heterosexual lives.

That is not to say we didn't have histrionics! We did. Girls fell in and out of love, there were jealousies and fights but this was part of life in a girls' borstal. I don't remember my colleagues and I thinking much of it. That was how it was. However, it could be problematic when it spilled over and involved staff. It wasn't unusual for borstal girls and indeed adult women to have 'a crush' or fall in love with staff members and I had my fair share of problems in this area.

I had returned to Bullwood Hall and took up my post as deputy governor after serving at Holloway and HM Borstal Hindley in Wigan. Babs was 17, young for her age, noisy and mouthy but lacking in any real self-confidence. She had a poor self-image. She had good friends amongst the girls but her relationships with her family, and indeed the majority of adults, weren't very good.

> I took my mam to the pictures last Friday (she paid herself in) she really showed me up. Just because it was eight bob to get in. She started telling everyone that when she was a kid she could get in for 3d. Then she started talking to me during the film. She drives me mad sometimes.

As deputy governor, I came into contact with all the girls, albeit for reasonably brief periods of time. But this didn't stop Babs developing a substantial crush on me. I didn't find it too difficult to cope with and the staff were supportive in helping Babs deal with her feelings. I felt it was important for Babs to develop good relationships with adults and learn to respect and be respected by adults. So we got on fine. But...

Everyone was rather shocked when Babs tattooed herself—with a big heart, a huge arrow and 'Babs loves Miss K' on her arm.

Tattooing was an offence against borstal discipline. The girls would somehow acquire biros—these were not allowed—draw their tattoos on their bodies and then prick in the ink with a pin. These became indelible and were hard-wearing—they were not easily removed. Girls who tattooed themselves in this way were stuck with their handiwork and sentiments for life albeit that the tattoo did fade with time.

I had done nothing to prompt Babs tattooing herself but I felt embarrassed. Here she was, scarred for life with my name prominently displayed if she chose to wear short sleeves. Fortunately for me and indeed for Babs, the psychiatrist who looked after the girls psychiatric needs, had started to remove girls tattoos surgically if they wanted this done, as part of the treatment available to them. A large number of borstal girls tattooed themselves — often inappropriately. Many had given themselves tattoos before they came into borstal and then found it difficult to live with what they had written — the names of old boyfriends, swear words and the like. Many grew to hate them.

> I really hate being outside. No jobs (and that's the truth) in this town. Well there's a lot of office work or shop work but I couldn't do work like that, even if I did have the brains. I don't they would accept me because of my arms and hands (I know it is all my fault) They're just the same. Mind you I really don't care what people think of me.

Girls needed to want their tattoos removed because it was a painful process — the medics needed to be convinced that they were ready to cope with the pain and that they would not just tattoo themselves again in a couple of days. The accepted way for the girls of removing a tattoo before this procedure became available, was by friction burn. Girls would rub their skin until it was raw — until the tattoo disappeared. This was hugely painful and easily became infected.

In time, Babs came round to the idea that she didn't need my name on her arm and it was removed. We remained good friends and she wrote to me often after she was discharged.

I met Gloria on borstal recall at Holloway. Gloria could be a real pain but she was often desperately upset and sad. She frequently 'cut-up' — cut her arms and legs with any sharp object she could find despite all our efforts to ensure she didn't have access to them. Slivers of glass picked up in the yard after someone had smashed their window and hidden well were difficult to find. Gloria was often prescribed medication — her choice — this helped her maintain some kind of equilibrium during her really bad times but she knew it wasn't the answer. With all her other problems she developed a crush on me but we managed to work this through on the wing in the group counselling sessions everyone attended. We moved through the stage where she would become silly when she saw me and even more so if we met — to seeing me as an adult friend to whom she could talk and chat. She wasn't much good at relating to adults particularly her family. After discharge from Holloway things didn't go well for her and she re-offended — as I remember it, trying to get back to Holloway where she had had positive experiences. But of course she wasn't sent back to borstal recall — she was given an adult sentence and sent to Styal Prison. She wrote to me from there.

November 16th

Hello Miss K

Gloria here. I thought it was about time I wrote to you and let you know how I'm getting on here.

Well for one thing I haven't had any reports yet and I intend to keep it that way. I work in one of the work rooms, and I make tassels for upholstery. Its really boring but I get 79p a week, that's top money. Not bad for me eh!

I'm on Fox House (one of the start houses) It's not bad. My best mate is here too. She's done recall, but not at the same time I was there. She done hers with Miss McFay.

I'll now tell you how we spend our days you probably know (but just in case you don't)

We rise at 6.30 and we have to sign the book before 7. Then from 7 till 7.30 we have a small job to do. we then have breakfast, then work, dinner and so on.

I haven't had any medicine since I've been here. I haven't cut my arms. When I think, I must have been mad. I wouldn't dream of doing it now. I've been here six weeks and don't I know it. I go home on the 12th. I've asked our Sally if I can go and stay with her for a while just till I get on my feet again, but I don't know what she'll say. If its no, then the Welfare officer wants me to go to a hostel in swinging Liverpool. I don't want to go but I suppose its better than walking the streets.

Do you remember Felicity, my Visitor? Well I still write to her. I really like her. I haven't heard from my mother, not that I'm really worried. She can get lost for all I care.

Remember the officer on Recall that cut everyone's hair. Well she cut mine. You should see it — short on top and feathered it's horrible. I hope its not too long before it grows again.

I'm in the same class as my best mate. Singing, gardening and family relationships. They are really boring but it passes the evening.

When I get out of here I'm really going to get a job and stick to it for as long as I can. I've made my mind up this time. Prison isn't like Borstal Recall.

When I left recall I felt lost because I could t speak to anyone like I used to speak to you and the other officers. I think that's why I got into trouble. (I really am mad)

I'm glad I'll be out for Christmas this year, although last Christmas on Recall was great. That was the best one I've ever had.

Will you give Miss Franks, Jollie (I really miss her) Bonnie and Freddie all my love and tell them I'm missing them like mad. I'm going to write to Freddie next week.

Well I'll finish for now and I'll write soon. Write when you have time (that's if you want to)

Good night God bless, all my love
Gloria

December 15

My dear Miss K

I thought it was about time I got my finger out and thanked you for your lovely letter which I was very pleased to receive.

Well since the last time you heard from me I've been in rather a lot of trouble. First I smashed a window and lost a week's pay. Then I ran out of the workroom and I lost 3 days remission, 3 days behind the door[5] and escort (that means I can't go anywhere in the prison without an officer) now I go home on 22 December. Well I'm not really bothered — it was all my own fault.

I'm sorry that Jollie didn't get her promotion. She's a senior officer and I suppose that's better than nothing.

The Welfare Officer wants me to go to a hostel in Liverpool but I've got somewhere else to go so she can stick the hostel.

Hows Miss Franks and Freddie keeping? Give them my love and tell them I might come to Holloway for a while. (I'm only joking)I'm going to try and stay out of trouble, well till after the new year!

---

5.   Locked in.

I'm glad you've got a magazine going on D Wing but I bet it won't be as good as the one Recall had eh?

I can't think of anything else to say except be good, give Jollie, Freddie and Miss Franks and everyone else my love.

God bless all my love
Gloria
Ps have a nice Christmas

Most relationships were all very innocent. The girls who professed love for me were needy and often unloved by their families. Many of them had driven their families away with their difficult disruptive behaviour. One might make a judgement on the way children had been brought up. Learning more about such parents from their daughters frequently exposed a continuous cycle of deprivation in which individuals lead their lives as best they could; more often than not they lacked role models, education, resources, and had little help or support; they frequently lived in grotty surroundings. With little hope and no positive expectations, it wasn't surprising that their children often ended up in a mess.

In most cases we didn't have these young women—although many borstal girls were more like children—for long enough to make a real difference. They left us and went back into the system outside and we had no further role in their lives. Looking back, I still find it heartbreaking that many of them had their best experiences of care and relationships in the penal system. Gloria talked about her best Christmas being on borstal recall. Boys were no different. Here is one of my borstal boys, Bill, writing from HMP Durham, commenting on Christmas:

Dear Joanna *(boys took far more liberties than the women and girls ever did!)*

Just a few lines to let you know that I am getting on OK. I received your Xmas card and it was very nice. In fact it was the only one I got this year. Well I hope this letter arrives to you in the best of health. Well I haven't received a letter from my father yet and he said he would come and see me before Christmas and he still hasn't come.

Bill and I corresponded off and on for about two years. He went from borstal to a local prison to Durham Prison. I suspect he grew into an 'old lag' — a real recidivist who couldn't survive outside a prison.

My role as assistant governor D Wing gave me responsibility for adult women for the first time and at age 26 this was quite a tall order. Adult women were not borstal girls and almost all of the women of the wing were older and maybe wiser in some respects than I. Nothing daunted, I threw myself into a new situation with enthusiasm. I believed that improving the quality of life for the women on the wing was an important part of my role. It seemed to me that women who were trying to rethink their lives in a positive way needed to be supported and encouraged.

Spreading the word about the magazine was important for me — I wanted as many people as possible to read it because I felt it presented a quite different image of women in prison. Women who were thoughtful, artistic and so normal. The magazine was something tangible they could be proud of. We sent copies to everyone we could think of. Myra was very helpful here because she knew many influential people. Most well-known amongst these was Frank Pakenham, Seventh Earl of Longford. I sent Lord Longford a copy of the magazine and received a kind reply:

Dear Miss Kozubska

Thank you so much for sending the first D Wing Magazine …As I told Myra I am delighted with it. I do heartily congratulate you on it and, if I may venture to say so, on all you are accomplishing.

Yours Sincerely,

Longford

It was easy to be impressed by Lord Longford's involvement with Myra and indeed that of prominent individuals. Myra needed all the friends she could get but as to the effectiveness of their interventions—who knows. Most of us felt that people such as Lord Longford only wanted contact with the most high profile prisoners and those convicted of the most serious offences. They did not appear to be overly interested in the run-of-the-mill everyday unknown women prisoners. These women might really have benefited from interventions by well-connected and powerful individuals. Help with rehabilitation and resettlement could well have born good fruit, particularly in influencing government.

Myra certainly could be manipulative and worked hard to get what she wanted. Which one of us in hopeless circumstances would not have done so? Myra's great problem was that her judgement was often very poor. Her involvement with Ian Brady has to be the best example of this. She trusted the wrong people; she frequently forgot that many people who were happy to become involved with her had their own vested interests which were normally more important to them then helping her. She was always seeking involvement with journalists for example, and failed to heed the warnings given to her. Interestingly, Lord Longford was probably the one person who didn't have a vested interest in the relationship. He withstood vicious criticism for his support of Myra but never wavered.

Suggesting that the women might like to write and produce a wing magazine was designed to give them some purpose and opportunity. It didn't occur to me that by allowing the women on D Wing to express themselves as they wished in this way and exercising no censorship, I was walking into a minefield, laying myself open to criticism. I didn't receive any advice or guidance from my seniors—I don't suppose that they even thought about any possible consequences of an innocuous wing magazine. They placed no restrictions on me or the magazine and consequently it was sent out to friendly folk. Some folk of course turned out to be not so friendly including an ex-inmate; she found ways to earn a bob or two I suspect.

We were cannon fodder for journalists. Brian McConnell, a seasoned journalist had a field day and it is a wonder that my prison service career didn't come to an abrupt halt as a result of a damning article he wrote for *Titbits*, a weekly magazine, now long deceased. McConnell was a tabloid journalist, a Fleet Street character, who some years later earned the Queen's Gallantry Medal for stepping between a gunman and the Princess Royal when her car was held up in The Mall. He was shot in the chest but survived. McConnell was very interested in the criminal fraternity and wrote about the Krays and other well-known villains.

MYRA
By Brian McConnell

Moors murderess Myra Hindley has been conducting the world's most extraordinary agony column — in a magazine for long term prisoners at Holloway women's jail, London. The magazine was closed down by the authorities after only two or three issues. And it's not hard to see why. Round the time it was appearing, Myra Hindley was involved in a lesbian relationship with a Holloway prison officer Pat Cairns, and her column is full of women-in-love jokes.

Betty Busybody was the name Hindley chose for herself. In nudge-nudge style she told readers 'If you've got a problem, don't hesitate to write to Betty Busybody. You can rest assured that you'll be more confused than ever when she's stuck her nose into your affairs'…

Famous Quotes

Apart from Betty Busybody's page there were articles by prisoners, a crossword, book reviews, a cookery column and apt aphorisms by the famous [people] such as Marcus Aurelius: 'Accept the things to which fate binds you and love the people with whom fate brings you together, but do this with all your heart.'…

McConnell goes on — quoting his source:

The idea of the agony column was put forward as a sort of joke. Myra's job was to empty the prisoners' suggestions box, and it was decided that she should use these in her column and supply the answers.

I understand it was this column with its over-riding emphasis on lesbianism that led the governor to stop publication after a few issues. The assistant governor, Joanna Kozubska, who has been moved to another prison, supervised the magazine. She was in charge of D Wing for long term prisoners, in which Myra Hindley is held.

The first editorial said: 'We are grateful to Miss Kozubska for sowing the seeds for the magazine and for her patient encouragement in our efforts to bring it to birth'.

Rather dishy

Nothing wrong with that. But Betty Busybody made rather more personal references to the assistant governor. This for instance:

Dear BB

I have fallen in love with the AG. Is this natural under the circumstances? Do you think you could feel the same way?

Bashful

Dear Bashful:

I think its natural under the circumstances; she is rather dishy. However, she censors this magazine. Would you write and inform your relatives of your immediate transfer to Dead-End Labour Camp, Siberia...

Here is another direct reference to her that leaves little doubt that Hindley was flirting with her in print:

Dear BB

Someone is queering my pitch! I've heard that they are in love with the AG. Well, I am too and I am most annoyed at their idea of a joke!

Jealous

Dear jealous: It's no joke; you and Bashful must learn to get along with each other. You're going to Siberia too.

This article appeared long after I had been transferred to HM Borstal Hindley. My transfer had nothing to do with the D Wing magazine. The magazine ceased because I was not on D Wing to support it. I remember being deeply shocked at the time. One of my colleagues sent me a copy of *Tit Bits*—I read it and put it away. Horrified. I couldn't read it again and I didn't until recently. Reading it now—knowing what our press sees as fair game and thinking about the damage that has been done to innocent people over the years I am deeply embarrassed at my naïvety and thankful that I escaped so lightly.

Fortunately for me no fuss was made about it, my responsibility for the magazine or anything else. I never knew if the powers that be read the article or not. I assume they did and decided to leave matters alone.

Today no doubt there would have been a real outcry. Heaven knows what I would be accused of! It never occurred to me then that people would read anything into what I considered to be just a lot of fun. But yes—I was naïve.

Recently I discussed this particular event with a good friend, an eminent criminal barrister, and we mused over the issues that it raised. He made the point that jealousies can and do arise when others covet a relationship particularly when that relationship is between an authority figure and one of their peers. I should not have been surprised that the person who I think might have given the story to Brian McConnell did so. There could well have been an element of jealousy here. I do have a number of letters from this individual, an example of which I include later.

My barrister friend followed up our conversation with a note:

> For long-term prisoners, as for all of us in life, unburdening can lead to under-standing and perhaps even to confession and redemption. But, in the closed circle of a prison to whom should anyone unburden themselves, or even take the first tentative steps in communication with an otherwise hostile world. There are consequences from a failure to communicate, but so also if those communications are misunderstood, particular if they are expressed in terms of a longing.

Dear Miss Kay

Sorry about the delay in writing to you but as you know the time slips by and it becomes months without realising it. I hope you are happy where you are

    I miss you a great deal to talk to' things have changed to the extent that I don't really know who lives on the wing any longer. Our new AG seems quite nice but once again I don't know her. May be in time as you would say? You will have heard by now that my parole was a mistake unfortunately. So I am to go for another review in a few months' time. But it's all gone over my head now so I shan't think of it. I wish you were still here but you're not so I'll just have to pack all the news into this letter. Jane is quite well. She keeps shouting at me — she says I am noisy at times. We both know that that's not true don't we (smile)the matron tried to take me quietly to the Obs the other day for being hysterical. I tried to convince her she was wrong and that I was joking. To be truthful, I got a bit panicky. Anyway she let me go in the end much to my gladness and her grief. Me and Mrs Kennedy keep laughing, also Miss Shepherd. They really make me laugh when they are together. My mum wants to send her regards to you. She is coming on Sunday. Miss Lever is taking me to buy some trousers so things can't be bad.

I am, still in the same old job making unnecessary tea. I don't see why they cant bring a flask, I did put the idea to them but they just ignored me so I am still running up 90 million stairs every day. I thought I was going to have to take to my bed after the parole but the call for tea came first (smile) Well Miss Kay, I really can't think of anymore news to tell you. I did hear that the boys are OK to you but don't think it could be the same. Down here there are millions of POUTS [Prison Officers Under Training] all over 90. Just screaming all over the place getting lost. It's terrible you wouldn't recognise the place. I really don't think I could ever come back to suffer it all again.

I have been out in the sun but as yet have not caught a tan. Somebody said I looked quite pale and ill. So I gave it all up. Caught hay fever out of the blue and I really don't like it.

I hope you have enjoyed this letter and please write back when you have the time. Take good care of yourself and don't forget to write millions of anonymous letters to the Parole Board on my behalf, I really do miss you and think of you often even though we did row but it was your fault so there. (smile)

Lots of love

Stephanie

PS I forgot to post this so it will arrive late. I went out with the Dep, Miss Lever, and bought some terrific clothes. Had a really nice time under the circumstances. At present I am bored to tears but tomorrow's another day.

Write soonest

Stephanie needed to talk a lot. About herself. At times she would also goad me by being anti-authority and yes — there were times I would get irritated and leave.

Dear Miss Kay

You left last night before I could tell you that if I upset you in anyway them I am really very sorry but I was feeling rather upset myself and felt sorry when you had gone. And I am immediately writing this and asking Miss French to leave this on your desk for you to read first thing in the morning.

Love
Stephanie xxx

A small number of female officers did have lesbian relationships but certainly not all. Husbands and boyfriends figured in conversations and appeared at various 'dos'. Many of the non-established officers — temporary officers as they were called then, had homes and families. As far as the same sex relationships went — no one batted an eyelid — if all was calm. Unlike most of the women and girls' relationships, these tended to be more serious long term ones, a lifestyle choice. Everyone, including the inmates, knew who was paired up with whom. No big deal. A prison is a closed community and when things went wrong — everyone knew about it. At Holloway and Bullwood Hall, officers were provided with accommodation as part of their package. And pretty poor accommodation it was. One tiny room little bigger than a cell, shared washing facilities and communal kitchen and recreation areas. Not surprisingly the officers' hostel could be a hothouse of emotion when things went wrong with a relationship.

Everything was played out in front of the community. Everyone knew what was going on. Just occasionally, an officer would over-react to an emotional crisis in the same way as a troubled borstal girl or indeed anyone outside. I remember one instance when one of my officers at Holloway refused to come out of her room, locked herself in and threatened suicide because her girlfriend had left her for someone else. All was resolved in the end but it was dicey at the time — no privacy for the officer or my conversations with her.

Female officers were treated very differently to the majority of their male counterparts and indeed to governor grade staff like myself in terms of the accommodation available for them. I always had good two-bedroomed accommodation — a flat outside the gates at Holloway; a beautiful flat in the old Edwardian mansion, Bullwood Hall, when I was the deputy governor there; a semi-detached house outside the wire when I was at Hindley Borstal. However, as a female assistant governor, I wasn't necessarily entitled to this. An extract from my letter of employment states:

> **Men Assistant Governors** are normally provided with unfurnished married quarters, which they are expected to occupy; an unmarried officer may occupy furnished bachelor accommodation when this is available, subject to the approval of the Department.

> **Women Assistant Governors** are provided with quarters which may consist of a suite of rooms; they are expected to occupy this accommodation, which may be furnished or unfurnished. Married quarters are not normally available for women Assistant Governors.

Officers were required to live in hostels but little thought was given at that time to the effect that such institutional living had on them. We were used to thinking about the effect of institutional living on inmates but it was more difficult to recognise it formally in the officer community.

Fortunately things did begin to change; two rooms were knocked together in the Bullwood hostel to give each officer a bedroom and a sitting room which made a huge difference to their lives. They had a tiny home rather than one room. Some officers started to move out to live in the community. As soon as the rebuilding started at Holloway, officers were moved out to other parts of London. The Prison Department rented houses already divided into flats for officers in Earls Court, and they began to lead more 'normal' lives — for example going to work by public transport like a large percentage of the population. These changes were greatly appreciated by the officers.

There were one or two officers who were definitely 'butch' — I can recall one particular woman, Eileen Greenaway. Off duty she wore a male three piece suit, shirt and tie and heavy shoes. On duty she wore uniform and her sexuality did not impinge on her work at all. She wasn't always easy could be negative in the extreme but she did respond to encouragement and opportunities to make a more positive contribution to the wing. Miss Greenaway was not unpopular with the women. They knew where they stood with her—she brooked no nonsense. In many ways she was a private woman but she would give away snippets of information about her background without knowing it. It seemed hardly surprising that she had become bitter; she came from an emotionally deprived background—unloved and unwanted by her parents. Perhaps because she knew from an early age that she was gay and made no bones about it as far as her family was concerned. Always different, always a figure of fun at school. Although she never explicitly admitted it—she had probably been raped as a young woman to make her 'normal'. Eileen had tried a number of jobs but these never last long. Eventually she found her way to the Prison Service and found a niche as a custodian. Trying to get her to work with the women in group work sessions was impossible but this wasn't surprising. Therapy even in this simplified form was too difficult for her—she appeared to share so many of the women's problems and anxieties and it wasn't surprising she shied away from any intimate discussions.

The officers I worked with at Bullwood and Holloway were caring women who did a good job, whatever their sexuality.

How did the women deal with their feelings of love and lost love? Let me borrow a phrase from McConnell's article—'in contrast to this mawkishness of style...'. What occasioned this critical description? He was referring to the poems that the women wrote and contributed to the D Wing magazines. He had quoted from a number which were obviously not to his liking.

Both the women on D Wing and the girls on Borstal Recall wing wrote poetry. Many of their poems focused on love, lost love and loneliness. Many were deeply saddened by events in their lives that had provoked intense emotions. Given the invitation and opportunity to write, some unburdened themselves and put their feelings onto paper. Some gave me copies of their poems because they were unable to say what they felt in an ordinary everyday way. It was easier to write poetry. Sometimes they would paraphrase a famous poet's work; sometimes they would adapt a well-known poem for themselves. Most wouldn't have had a clue about plagiarism—they just wanted to express what they felt—and share it with others. The *Oxford Shorter*

English Dictionary tells us that 'mawkish' means 'imbued with sickly or false sentiment'. Some of their poetry might not be particularly good poetry but McConnell was quite wrong. The sentiment was always real.

Ode On the Death of a Broken Heart

As the wind whispers silently through the trees,
I softly tread down the lanes of memories,
Looking into the very depths of my immortal soul,
Wondering why in my heart I am bitter and cold,
Lost in the grey swirling mists of the times,
I hear sweet voices speaking to me always lies,
My brain is reeling and my mind is a blank,
The waves of fear pound over me and still I sank,
Down into the lonely depths of despair,
Looking for my love but will he be there,
My body doth sleep forever my journeys and nears,
Heavy is the bleeding heart who holds your image to it so dear
Still weary for one last kiss, ere my crushed spirit passes
through those open gates,
Your sweet voice challenges, tells my body to awake and for
soul to return, but the dark hand of death is the stronger,
Your love for me relives, alas too late.

By Emily Blackthorn

Typed on a small piece of buff paper, folded in quarters with Miss K written in pencil on the blank side. It wasn't written to me—it was written to help me understand Emily's feeling of loss and desolation. Her man wasn't going to be there for her when she got out, he had made that clear when she was sentenced to five years. He wasn't going to wait. Writing this poem helped Emily to talk about her future which looked dark without him.

What is love? The Poets say,
Intangible in every way.
I think that love is very sad,

and wonderful, and also mad.

As my love and I have found such bliss

Without even touch or any kiss.

I long for your arms to hold me tight,

And take always all the fears

That life and time have created

For us with much strife.

But my love, this cannot be yet,

As you and I have still not met.

A poem written for Borstal Recall Magazine

The temptation is to change the words to improve the poem. But why do this? I suspect we all know what the writer means.

An example of a letter from Myra Hindley to the author

o↙
½

In replying to this letter, please write on the envelope:—

Number.964.055... Name...H.I.N.D.L.E.Y........ m

Posted Mon., 16/12/74.

H.M. PRISON,
PARKHURST ROAD,
HOLLOWAY,
LONDON N.7

Dear JK,

Can I still address you thus, in view of your promotion? (smile) Congratulations are somewhat belated, but nevertheless sincere, from all of us who were on D-Wing when you were (aeons ago!)   ?. I know I should have written sooner – I think I last wrote in May or thereabouts, to Wigan – but until Nov., 5th I was working hard on the Course, preparing for the exam – which was simply awful   and I did it together; she did Social Sciences and I did Humanities. I threw my pen down three times, but and Richard bullied me into carrying on. I'm convinced I've failed – we won't know until January – but I'll still be able to go on to next year's Course, an amended version of this year's Social Sciences; this year it was called Understanding Society and next year it will be Making Sense of Society, which is more in my line (smile). It's another Foundation Course, for I'm doing an Honours and have to do two Foundations. So I can re-sit the Humanities exam. next year, for I've passed on my assignment grades over this year, and they constitute half of the marks. Although I'd like to have done with it, I'd rather fail and do better next year, instead of only just scraping through, for when one has completed the Degree, a first or second class Honours depends on the percentage of exam. marks.

No. 243 30141 8-2-68

I must pass both next year, in order to move up to a second level course, which will be, in my case, the Age of Revolutions. I hope to do a ½ credit course along with that one, the Fall of the Roman Empire and the Rise of Christianity ___ has to pass this exam, because she's registered for a second level course next year, and I'm sure she will pass. She's on F-wing now, next door to me. We shared her cell for 4 days before the exam, burning the midnight oil each night, tables strewn with books and endless black coffee. And cigarettes — I've started smoking again. We also share during lunch and tea-time lock-up, which is better than being alone. We've become addicted to Scrabble, and I keep telling her she's the nearest thing to being a cheat without actually being one. I've just told her what I've written, and she said ___ censored!

I've got myself together again after months of complete hell. I thought for a time that I'd be unable to do so, for I don't think I've ever felt so utterly low and helpless in my entire life before, but I guess resilience is part of my make-up. (an adjective someone else applied to me many months ago, and not for the first time, either) I've often hated myself before but this time I hated myself so much, I could hardly live with myself. I still haven't completely purged all the hate away, but enough of it to have been able to partly come to terms with myself and life. I can't attribute that to time, for unfortunately, time sometimes stands still; it must be the urge for self-preservation. During that prolonged period, I often used to think of steel, in order to derive inspiration or whatever. I'm glad I read up the processing of it, for I remembered all the stages it had to go through

before all the impurities and everything were eradicated. I must
be one of those pieces which have to keep going back
into the furnace, and I certainly leapt in there myself this
time (smile)

We've organised another choir this Christmas, singing two or
three of the carols we sang in your choir, and about half a dozen
others. We'll be singing at the Carol Service on the 23rd, and will
also go round the wings on Christmas Eve, when we hope to borrow
some surplices (there are just over a dozen of us). Mrs. Stern
suggested making some out of red crepe paper, but it will rustle
too much, and anyway, someone said 'Well, I'm not prancing
around in a sheet of paper!' so that settled it. It's very sad
about Mrs. Stern. She's been organising this for a few months
now, and we were meeting every Thursday lunch-time, but she's gone
into the Royal Northern today (Mon.) to have her gall-bladder
removed, and will be in over Christmas. We'll send her a card and try
to have the Service recorded for her, for she's been so patient with
us. (you'll remember how temperamental Holloway choirs are? (smile)
I know she'd love to hear from you, which is why I've mentioned it to
you. A nice girl named Melanie is coming in every day from tomorrow
to help, and will probably bring some 'modern' stuff with her. She
came in October, and we did excerpts from Jesus Christ Superstar
and some of our own things too. It was quite a success. A few of
us, myself and Anna included, entered the Kettle Music Award thing,
and Anna and I won prizes for singing with guitars. I sang a Bob
Dylan song, recorded by Joan Baez, Love Minus Zero/No Limit, and
the judges remarks were: Words very good, so was breath control.
This had a folk quality, and the singer made me want to listen.
~~They~~ You sing well in tune. There was a strange purity of

expression here, which though unusual, was rather compelling. A good performance.' — If it wasn't on just a strip of paper, I'd frame it. (smile) Two men from Radio London came to record us, and they were so nice, they put us at our ease right away. All the 'machinery' was out by the Chaplain's office, and only a couple of 'mikes' were in the chapel. They said they'd play the winning pieces on Radio London, and would let us have a rough idea of the time, etc, but they played my piece on the World At One, from a collected tape of prison entries, anonymously, of course.

I'm quite worried. I haven't heard from her since October 1st, and at that time, she'd been charged for cultivating a marijuana plant, found in the house when the police raided it (dressed as hippies, with headbands and flowers and bells and the works!) I wrote a couple of weeks ago, and will write again before Christmas, so I hope she's okay, and not in the County Jail, which her P.O. recommended for violation of her probation. She lost your address yet again, and asked me to send it. Since then you'd moved to Bulwood, so I'll send the address when I next write. I'll have to get it myself in order to post this.

I must close in a moment. For the first time in ten Christmases I've decided not to send any cards, except home, so Christmas and New Year wishes, lots of good ones, come with this letter. How is your Mother keeping? Well, I hope, and of course I hope you are, too. I'm so pleased about your new job, for I imagine you are much happier there. My mother and Maureen are coming this Saturday. Haven't seen mum since Sept., so I'm looking forward to the visit. I'll write again in the New Year, and hope to hear from you meanwhile. God bless for now. Everyone sends love and best wishes. Love, Myra

Myra Hindley wrote close to the edge of the page top, bottom and sides.

CHAPTER 9

Families Left Behind

June 1973

Dear Miss K

We were so touched to think that you took the trouble to ring up a week ago to ask about Naomi. We have been worried about her after she fell down the stairs in prison.

She hadn't sent us a letter as she was waiting for a visiting order—and as you know stamps are precious and have to be horded. I finally had a note yesterday and I am going to see her next week.

Naomi wrote in her note that it was extremely hot in her cell and that if she hadn't washed her hands at frequent intervals her white embroidery would have been a dirty mottled grey. Anyway I'll write another note to you in a few days when I have more news to give you.

Leaving Brighton today about six am was sad; blue blue sea; a well cut expanse of green lawn; flowerbeds full of roses and antirrhinums, and three reproachful pussies watching the car depart. I've left the fridge full of food to tide my three men and three cats over until I return in a couple of days.

Please please come and see us whenever you can. We'd be most pleased to see you at any time. We are more grateful for your support than words can express.

Sincere good wishes for your new post.

Susan Jarvis

July

Dear Miss K

The Appeal process was much delayed and it has been a hard fight this has upset Naomi a great deal. But all the authorities have been very kind. Naomi has not recovered well from her fall and Sister McGill on the Hospital wing was marvellous.

When I do see Naomi I am not the best of companions as I get so fraught myself. I worry so much. I don't like going home to face friends and neighbours. I'd rather crawl into a tiny anonymous hole and hide away. However I must make myself go back home soon.

I'll write again soon. Meanwhile very many thanks for your call. You are so good to us and we are most grateful always.

Yours very sincerely

Susan Jarvis

August 1973

My Dear Joanna (If I may)

I am ashamed when I look at the date on your letters for which I was very grateful—though you wouldn't think it with this delay.

I came back from my last visit to Naomi in a dreadful state. I spent about ten days in a daze—valium etc feeling very ill. But friends came and suggested we pop over to France for the day which we did. The weather was wonderful—it did me the world of good. I've stopped the pills and pulled myself together.

The weather has been marvellous and I do hope it will continue for all those people on their holidays down here. We live quite near Brighton beach so we see them all the time. And it is so miserable for them, when it rains!

I paused to re read your letter. I'd like to think that you are enjoying your new post more now. Do you know convents do the same thing? As soon as a person is doing too well in a perfectly fitting job they move that individual. I worked with nuns for some years and it seemed such a stupid policy to me. Lancashire is such a lovely county and I am sure you will get to know it well.

My men are enjoying the sun — plenty of cricket in this glorious weather. I have to watch what I say to them and to friends. I don't think I will ever feel free again in my life — of suspicion. How we came to be in this situation.

Yours affectionately, Susan Jarvis

November

My Dear Joanna

(am I allowed to address you as thus? Even 'Miss K' seems a bit formal for the warm feelings we have for you through Naomi)

Your letter was awaiting us from a brief stay in Spain last month. I had gone to pieces — as a result of nervous exhaustion in the summer after the Appeal. I was beyond having visitors or writing letters for a good many weeks. Then I picked myself up and tucked my depression firmly away and began to get back to normal life again. We had a lovely week of sun and sea flowers, local food and the fun of coping with an unknown language which I always enjoy.

I feel nothing but gratitude for the kindness of all the authorities. The Governor, Deputy Governor, and all those connected with Naomi's appeal. They have been wonderful. I admire Naomi tremendously for her courage and honesty. She gained everyone's respect including her parents. I still think of her life as ruined. How can she come back from the awful truth of the lives she has ruined through her association with the serious criminal fraternity involved in drug smuggling and distribution. I wish I were safely out of life, having no desire to go on living...no hope for the future. Apart from that permanent and fundamental feeling I'll plod on and do the best I can for Naomi. I shall never let her know how I feel of course.

I am writing under difficulty at the moment. Three cats are fighting to sit on my lap and they are not taking kindly to my leaning my writing pad on them.

Do you know, the atmosphere of the part of Spain we were in is so old fashioned. People, the poorer financially, worked contentedly at their jobs. There was no strain and stress, no feeling of greedy grabbing and cut throat competition. And the school population—neat clean and orderly went about their business—the boys distinguishable from the girls by hair style, clothing—(though many of the girls did wear neat slacks) and all so wholesome looking somehow. But I mustn't launch into criticism of our youth. After Naomi's failure I can never criticise or offer and opinion again. I am so deeply ashamed, that I'll never face the people in our local area again. They all know who I am. I have cut myself off from Church and the Library and the local shop. I shop further away now. (My fault—people are always so kind and friendly if I do bump into anyone I know) so I must say nothing about the youngsters of today.

Oh dear! I hope this letter hasn't been a dirge. I have neglected all my friends because I have found it impossible to write without sounding depressed…and it isn't fair to inflict that on other people, because everyone has problems and most people have the courage to cope with them.

I wonder how you have settled in the north. I hope its getting more interesting for you. But how I wish you were back in the London area and available for us to see from time to time.

I walked along the front yesterday looking at all the people wrapped up—the sea grey, flat calm with warmth in the air and a golden path of light of the setting sun on the water. A beautiful scene and a beautiful walk. Yet by the weekend that sea may be roaring and raging and pounding the pier—which is why I love living by the sea with its ever changing mood. Come and see it for yourself when ever you need a break. You know how warmly we'd welcome you.

Please write when you have time and inclination

Yours-in-a-twist
Susan Jarvis.

I didn't visit Susan Jarvis. This is the last letter I have from her.

August 1972
Dear Miss Kabutska

Thank you very much for all you have done and are doing for my daughter Pippa. It was very kind of you to arrange this week's home visit and she really appreciated it and was able to sort out one or two problems, see Frank etc

Your job must be a most exhausting and demanding one and I really admire you for doing it in the atmosphere of a prison — full of anxious & suspicious people — must be depressing and you must have a vocation for it.

I hope you will continue to keep in touch with Pippa as she takes notice of what you say! I am too emotionally involved and she probably considers me old-fashioned and staid, in any case she does not want any more 'lectures' from me.

It has been a trying time but the in-laws and myself have kept the home going so she has somewhere decent to come back to. It will be good for her to see her twins, Sally & Susie, again as this has been a bitter deprivation and I think their company should have a softening effect.

I am very fond of Pippa but I cannot understand her, also her violent language & unrestrained emotions give me a pain in the solar plexus — but I think that she will alter once she mixes with normal people in normal surroundings — frustration has to be worked off against <u>somebody</u>. She has so many good qualities and has a very likeable and charming side.

Please feel free to phone me anytime

Always yours sincerely and gratefully
Betty Rothwell

October 1972
Dear Miss Kaboustka

Re: Pippa French
I wrote you a little while ago about my daughter, and have tried to phone you in the evening so far without success. I feel you understand her, and have a good relationship with her, and I truly value your opinion and understanding.

As the time for her release draws near, I am, very concerned for the twins future. I feel that until Pippa is more settled they will face a very uncertain and bewildering, even unhappy time with her. She is so insecure and so much an 'unstable' child herself, and the dangers of drugs, poverty, unfortunate associates etc are great, also she is not a 'maternal' person.

I feel deeply for her in many ways; she has such a good side (largely untapped) and has had much ill fortune, and not having seen her twins and her husband save in brief, sad snatches which has been a terrible punishment (largely unmerited I feel- her offence being largely a 'technical' one) she is however, very selfish, wild, headstrong and unstable, and shows some psychopathic tendencies — i.e an inability to form permanent relationships, lack of foresight, desire for immediate satisfaction — and a Jekyll & Hyde personality.

I am being asked to testify against her re the care of her twins and by her solicitor for her! I cannot adequately describe the agony this causes me.

I love her deeply but see disaster ahead unless she changes; but she must have her <u>chance.</u> Disinterested love; 'patience' and understanding drugs, imprisonment, marriage to another psychopathic personality have caused deterioration but there <u>is</u> hope — and with <u>expert</u> help who knows -?? There is so much good (loyalty, honesty, courage, humour.) She might turn round like St Francis!!

Could you get in touch with me and advise me? She listens to you, It is the twins welfare that concerns me vitally at this time

Yours sincerely
Betty Rothwell

Home Office
HM PRISON
Parkhurst Road Holloway London N7

3 10 72

Dear Mrs Rothwell

Thank you for your letters. I must apologise for not having replied to your earlier letter — I have been in rather a dilemma. Technically, my responsibility for Pippa ends when she is released from here but I have been finding it increasingly difficult to justify in my own mind such an action. One cannot just abdicate the responsibilities of a relationship built up over several months — one which has much value on both sides.

I agree with everything you said of Pippa in your letters and I can well understand the difficulties you are experiencing at this moment. I fear that the future will not be easy for either of you.

I imagine that it will not be possible for you to visit Pippa before her release next week. I feel I should have suggested a welfare visit beforehand. If you or Pippa felt that I could be of help I would be most happy to come and see you both when I am at home. I do not live far from you. Perhaps you would like to telephone me after 7pm when we could arrange to meet if you would find this helpful.

Please forgive me for not taking the initiative; it in no way means that I am not interested.

I look forward to meeting again

Yours sincerely

Joanna Kozubska

October 1972

Dear Miss Kozubska

Thank you very much for your helpful (and indeed hope-giving) letter.

We will certainly get in touch with you. Thank God you live so near.

My own inclination is not to testify in court at all (a clever solicitor could tie me in knots) a plague on both their houses — I do know that at the bottom Pippa does love her twins and she has been deprived of everything that makes life worth living for a long time — but at the same time she is like a demanding child herself and very irresponsible and will need a lot of help (?NACRO, Samaritans? Drug Offenders society) She has a poor relationship with her Probation Officer who seemed rather authoritarian and unsympathetic — poor woman, I expect her case load is too heavy.

The time ahead will present difficulties but Pippa's inlaws are good, steady, kind people and I have great faith in God who manifests himself most of all at such times as these.

Bless you and thank you

Yours sincerely

Betty Rothwell

November 1972

Dear Joanna

Just a line — I have a few minutes to spare in between jobs — to thank you again. But for you Pippa would have been hardened and embittered I think. As it is, in many ways there is a great improvement. She has learned some patience, tolerance and pity for others. Also it is touching that she phones me very regularly (sometimes too regularly — as I am regaled with every item of news, regardless)

She was thrilled to get a nice letter from you and has bombarded me with breathlessly enthusiastic comments etc!!

On Monday she started work in the local department store. £216 per week and I hope she will part let her house to someone who will share the overheads.

I hope you will see her over the weekend if you can generously spare an hour of your valuable time, especially if the twins are there — you will be able to form your own conclusions.

It is asking a lot of you in the circumstances but we both know the value of trust and discretion.

In a way I think this period on her own without Frank will be very good for her character and will help her to see things clearly.

She seems to have a lot of men friends, but she is forewarned and wary of those who are merely out for what they can get. She has become quite tough and sophisticated and will I think, be able to form quite wise judgements as to who is/are her real friends, and well intentioned.

Loads more I could say. But there are jobs waiting my attention.

I have given up reproaching myself as a mother, we do our best but this is an odd world we live in and we all have to make mistakes. This is how we progress. I am not religious in the formal sense but though this suffering, have been vouchsafed glimpses of a world beyond this — by grace as it were — worth all this pain, with many thanks again. God bless you

Yours

Betty (Rothwell)

I visited Pippa on a number of occasions on the understanding that she had no drugs in the house. I stopped visiting when she told me, in a fit of bravado, that she had hidden drugs behind the light switches.

June 1973

Dear Miss Kozubska

Now that you have left Holloway I am confident that I am breaking only a minimum of the Prison Regulations by writing to you to thank you for all you did for Mattie.

These last ten months have been very frustrating for her. But they could have been very much worse from what I have learnt, and from my own contacts with you. I am absolutely confident that it was very largely due to your help and encouragement, and your willingness to short circuit useless red tape, that this period wasn't very much worse. If we are ever able to look back on this period, and feel that on balance it was profitable, rather than sterile — and I think we may — that it will have been very much due to you. Thank you very much.

I was particularly anxious to write because I understand your activities have been cruelly rewarded. I want you to know that all you were able to do was greatly appreciated in at least one quarter, and your courage and persistence greatly admired. I do hope you will not think me impertinent or pompous in writing this!

We hope that Mattie comes home on parole very soon; her folks and I can't wait.

We are looking forward to meeting you again quite soon — under happier circumstances.

Once again, thank you for all that you did,
Yours sincerely

Paul Finley

6 August

Dear Joanna

This is just a sad little note to say that we weren't able to visit you as soon as we had hoped.

Incredibly, Mattie has been refused parole. I won't bore you with my views on the ultra secretive Parole Board. Suffice it to say that I and everyone concerned with Mattie at Holloway, am surprised and upset. Mattie had so expected parole at an early date that she is cruelly disappointed. Needless to say she is taking the decision very well. I have learned to respect and love her even more over the last few days — she is superb under extreme distress and is a comfort to me, who has so much less to cope with.

There does not seem to be any chance of a change of heart, but we are not taking the decision without protest. I have drafted a letter to the Secretary of State but I don't think there is a chance in a million that there will be any change.

I hope your new job is going well. we will be up to see you as soon as we can.

Incidentally, the not-too-bad development is 5 days Home Leave for Mattie as from August 18th. These <u>will</u> be <u>very</u> good days!

Best wishes

Paul

20 September

Dear Joanna

This is partly to thank you — very belatedly — for your good advice as to parole and partly because a short-of-letters Mattie asked me to let you know how she is getting on.

There is no progress at all about Parole. We have written to the Secretary of State both directly and through my MP but we have not even had the courtesy of a reply. I have no doubt that a few days after release we will get a curt little letter saying that the Board has reconsidered its decision but can see no reason to change it.

But you will know far more about the workings of the Parole Board and its red tape than we do. Thank God we will be rid of it all in 96 days, 8½ hours precisely! At least we have reached the stage when it is meaningful to cross days, not just months, off the calendar.

Mattie is taking more home leave in October and we have booked a cottage in the Brecon Beacons. I am sure it will be a healthy and relaxing break but I confess to worrying a little that it will be a bit cold and damp for Mattie. I don't see why she should be any the worse for it though! There will be an open fire and plenty of sweaters and exercise. And if the weather is poor, we don't have to go anywhere. We just stay put or walk down to the pub and watch nature all around us. Might be a bit bleak in October but it won't matter.

How are your 'boys'? Did you go to any of the conferences at York, where it seemed that everyone in the penal field was there? I was greatly heartened to read authoritative criticisms of the secretive Parole procedure, and also the sentencing abilities of certain members of the judiciary. Perhaps, who knows, within the next 20 years or so, there will grow up a system under which custodial sentences will be applied and maintained only where they are actually useful and profitable. But I doubt it!

All best wishes
Paul

I met Paul regularly when he visited Mattie but I don't think I ever met them outside prison.

July 24th
Dear Miss 'K'

We appreciated your kind letter and we would like say that people like you are so precious in our Prison Service

I for one understand how frustrating it can be to see so many human problems, and yet feel so suffocated about the end result, but one must go on slowly but surely getting results. Hazel's sentence is so long — fifteen years but we can not give up.

We would be so pleased if you would visit us when you can. Our phone number is xxxxxx Please let us know when you have time available and then we can get together on a date suitable for all of us.

We can then have a good chat –

Looking forward to seeing you when ever

Yours sincerely

Janie Peterson

Ps Hazel's grandparents went to visit her last Sunday for the first time. The prison were indeed very good and gave them nothing but kindness — and made it all much easier for them to bear. (Thought you would like to know)JP

1 October

Dear Joanna

Thank you for your letter — interesting to hear you attended the conference. I feel I would like to interest myself in the subject but feel at the moment I have my own pressure group going in that field.

Hazel has not been so well lately. She has had a bad chest infection which is pulling her down. She also has trouble with her teeth — her gums are tender and shrinking — the dentist says nothing can be done — the soggy food. Hazel is used to fresh fruit etc and of course she is not getting the food that is necessary for her health. Obviously her chest and constant antibiotics, the stresses and strains are not helping.

I made an appointment to see the doctor and the Governor. I had about 30 minutes with the doctor — she is a very human person. I then saw the Governor about Hazel's welfare — to constantly keep in touch with both the doctor and the Governor is my primary concern — I feel Hazel must have as much support as possible to cope with this punitive sentence. I don't want to see her deteriorate in any way bodily or mentally. She is too much of a person for that; she has thought too much of other people and not enough of herself in the pat. She must now concentrate on her own survival if she can. it's the only way. She has much love to give and love and so — we hang on tight — always until she is free.

How's your work going? Do keep in touch.
Janie Peterson

Ps love to Hazel when you see her and let me know how things are—thanks for
your friendship
JP

I visited the Petersons once at their home. It was a strange but enjoyable experience. Sitting chatting with Hazel's parents while their daughter
was locked up many miles away was somewhat surreal. Her parents were
delightful and I felt that I would always be able to go and see them if I wanted
to. They made no excuses for their daughter's behaviour; they loved her dearly
and intended to stand by her as she worked through a long sentence. They
longed for parole for her.

As I look back now I still continue to be surprised that, on occasions, I
appeared to matter to the relatives of women in my care. None more so than
the daughter of one of the women I got to know well at Holloway, Rachel.
Her daughter was Ruth.

London
25th May

Dear Miss 'K'

I really don't know what to say to you or write because what I've heard from
my mother you seem to know everything about me, so there wont be much
I can tell you.

Anyway how are you? I want to say thank you very very much for you
helping my mother and looking after her.

I feel I want to go back to Israel. I also feel that its my country but I know its
impossible for me to go back at least until I'm over 18 'That's life' I've learned a
lot by all this and in some ways and I'm thankful in other ways.

May be I can see you in the near future, maybe with Mum.

Now I am settled and ready to start a commerce course at school. I hope I can make a start on a new life.

Thanks yours
Ruth

Her mother wrote

I saw Ruth this evening and she showed me your letter with great pride and surprise that you bothered to write to her after what she had done. She has replied already , so I will no tell you her news, will let you read it for yourself. Suffice it to say that she seems to be settling down.

London
19.6.73

Dear Miss 'K'

I was really pleased to have received your letter. I thought may be you had left Holloway before the letter had arrived.

Since my last letter many things have happened to me. I don't know whether I told you but I started school again. After being there a week it was seen that I couldn't settle down. I was playing truant after a lot of screaming and shouting, phone calls etc it was decided that I wouldn't go to school but would start at Secretarial College, not a school. I'm not sure which one. I have to visit quite a few but this is what I really want, after being in Israel, independent, I found it so hard to go back to school.

I didn't know you were going to a borstal. What's it like? Do you ever get involved with the boys? Is it upsetting? What you did say about them, it seems quite sad. Do they do what they do because they are not cared for and loved? What ages are they?

My mother is fine, working hard and enjoying her freedom, funnily enough I will be seeing her tonight. We all had a wedding on Sunday. My brother and mother went but I didn't. I know that I wouldn't have felt right.

I have a Holloway magazine here and have read it. Congratulations. I think its really good and I've learn't quite a bit about life. As you said in your letter 'you don't have to learn everything by experience.'

Well, I wish you luck with your boys and hope you've got your last curtains up by now!!

Well write back

Best wishes

Ruth

PS I am sure my mother will want me to say she sends her regards!

C Wing—One of the six prison wings, housing the hospital on the first two
floors and the remand centre on the third and fourth floors

CHAPTER 10

Rooftops and Barricades, Riots and a Horse Race

The BBC evening news led with film of several of my borstal recall girls from DX Wing sitting on the roof of the prison throwing shoes at the Governor—shouting that their assistant governor was being moved unfairly and that they didn't want this to happen. A few minutes later the phone rang. A cool-voiced, rather distant deputy governor informed me that I must not return to DX Wing but should go immediately to D Wing on Monday morning. A hasty call to one of my colleagues on duty that weekend revealed all. There were photos in many of the national papers the next morning. Friday had been 'a bad day at the office'.

I had been posted to HMP Holloway following my eight months training at the Prison Service Staff College in Wakefield and took up my role as assistant governor II in change of the Psychotherapeutic Wing for borstal recall girls with enthusiasm.

There were less than 20 girls on DX Wing; all had been recalled to borstal because they had broken the terms of their borstal licence. This would have meant that they had re-offended, behaved badly, or taken themselves off to places other than those agreed with their probation officers.

What did psychotherapeutic mean? Every morning we had a meeting where wing business was discussed but more importantly where the girls were encouraged to talk about their problems with the group—staff and the other girls on the wing. The wing psychiatrist and I ran these daily sessions. The psychiatrist saw each girl individually as well—if she wished.

I really enjoyed this work. I took to it like a duck to water. Indeed, I was passionate about it. The girls could be difficult, some were disturbed,others had just been a pain on the outside and found themselves recalled because people couldn't be bothered with them or didn't have the necessary time to invest in the support needed to keep them on the straight and narrow. These youngsters were a challenge in every way but I liked them and enjoyed good relationships with them.

Sally, released on borstal licence just after Christmas in 1977, wrote:

Deperty Governer

Thank you for having them torks with me, I am very greatfull for it. I wish I did all my sentens at Bullwood.

I no before Christmas I make a fuss about not going but I am sorry for that. I am very thankfull to you and all the staff on house one. Will you say thank you for me. I wish I didnt have to go from there because I am very depressed.

Wish I was still there. I dont like it in this world because it is to big and to complacated. I just don't now what to do with myself. I am confused with everything.

I hope you will not show this to anyone else.

Please let me now if you get this letter.

I think borstal did help a bit.

Signed S Hampton Thank you

Instances of disturbed behaviour occurred both easily and spontaneously. 'Cutting-up' or self-harming, as we would say now, could be quite distressing. Borstal trainees smashing-up their cells, destroying their meagre possessions was not an uncommon response to overwhelming or unmanaged emotions. This spontaneous crazy place was my world and I felt I was making a difference to the lives of those in my care. I was involved, some might say over involved. I cared deeply about all those girls and my team of committed staff.

Jane offended again after being released from borstal recall and served her sentence at Styal Prison. The full text of her letter, parts of which I quoted earlier, reads:

I haven't had any medicine since I've been here. I haven't cut my arms. When I think—I must have been mad. I wouldn't dream of doing it now. I've been here six weeks and don't I know it. I go home on 21.12.72. I've asked our Florrie if I can go and stay with her for a while. Just till I get on my feet again, but I don't know what she will say...........when I get out of here I'm really going to try as hard as I can to get a job and stick to it for as long as I can. I've made my mind up this time. Prison isn't like Borstal Recall. When I left Recall I felt lost because I couldn't speak to anyone like I used to talk to you and the other officers. I think that's why I got into trouble. (I really am mad) I am glad I will be out for Christmas although last Christmas on Recall was great. That was the best Christmas I ever had. Will you give Miss Brown, Poppy, Miss Franks and Hattie all my love and tell them I am missing them. I will write to Poppy next week.

Well I'll finish for now and I'll write every soon. Write when you have time (that's if you want to).

Goodnight God bless. All my love.
Jane

Things didn't go well for Jane despite her determination to make everything work. Four weeks later she wrote:

My Dear Miss K

I thought it was about time I got my finger out and thanked you for your lovely letter, which I was very pleased to receive.

Well since last time you heard from me, I've been in rather a lot of trouble. First I smashed a window and lost a weeks pay. Then I ran out of the workroom and lost 3 days remission, 3 days behind the door and escort.(That means I can't go anywhere in the prison without an officer) now I go home on the 22 December. Well I'm not really bothered—it was all my own fault.

Despite having a family, Jane appeared to prefer the more secure and caring environment of borstal and prison. Desperately sad, but a fact of life for so many of the young women I knew. We made a difference to the girl's lives while they were with us but undoing the damage crafted by years took a lot longer than a borstal term which was normally months not years. I hope we gave them some respite. However, the contrast was often so great that life inside was a more attractive proposition than the uncertainty and insecurity of life in the community.

Back to my 'bad day in the office' …

Every morning at 9.30am the Governor held a meeting for the medical officer, deputy governor, assistant governors and chief officer—we referred to this as the Governor's 'knitting circle'. Here, the business of the day was discussed; we shared information and the Governor gave her instructions. On that fateful Friday morning—out of the blue—the Governor announced that she was rotating the assistant governors and, as part of this exercise in musical chairs, I was to move to D Wing for long-termers and lifers in two weeks' time.

I was aghast, devastated and upset.

I returned to the wing and the morning group meeting. Unable to hide my feelings, I told everyone. The trainees were upset and felt aggrieved. The staff present, the psychiatrist, Zdenka Pick (our wing probation officer) and I, tried to work the girls through this. I felt we had done so and, saddened, I left for my weekend off and drove home to Dorset.

The weekend was ruined. I spent a miserable couple of days waiting for news that the girls had come down—whilst at the same time envisaging their punishment.

The Governor was furious. Head office was not amused. Each girl was charged under borstal regulations, found guilty and had her release date delayed by several months. Those girls knowingly extended their imprisonment for me as a result of my error of judgement. They only came down from the roof because Zdenka Pick, climbed up 30 feet on a rickety ladder to talk to them (fortunately no health and safety in those days). She told them that things would be even worse for me and them if they did not come down.

It was a big mistake. Though counselled not to, I had behaved in exactly the same way as the trainees—I failed to stop and think about the consequences of my actions. I failed to control my own emotions. And, just as for them, things turned out badly for a number of people including myself. These girls served an extra six months for my mistake. The next few weeks were difficult. I talked to my colleagues—of course I did, but I didn't feel they understood. I was upset that the Governor had made the decision she had and communicated it in the way she did. This was balanced by the knowledge that the trainees both cared for and appreciated me. One of my colleagues feels that borstal girls did anything for attention and to cause problems but I think that is unfair.

Kim wrote from Moss Side Hospital:

Dear Miss K

Many thanks for the letter which I received yesterday. I had a letter and a couple of Mars Bars off Billy [the senior officer on the Borstal Recall Wing] on Wednesday. I wrote back yesterday.

It was in the paper about you being moved to another wing. I am glad that I'm not still at Holloway because I would have been very upset to see you moved.

Not yet a year in post, unfortunately, I'd already come to the notice of my superiors. One of my male colleagues wrote to me:

4th May 1972

Dear Jo

What a crazy letter this is likely to be, since I have little idea of how to express what I would like to say. I have been reading in the gutter press (ie Daily Express) of the girls response to your transfer. I knew little else except that Christine tells me that you have not been treated in the most sympathetic manner.

Jo — have confidence. At all times demonstrate the integrity I know you have shown since you have been at Holloway. The service appears loaded against the thinking person. Still think, and still act. Have the courage to pursue your ideas. What if the institution does not appreciate motives — institutions are not people, but organisations of people. Be yourself. People do not attain the respect you have earned by being inefficient. Be happy.

Peter

As instructed, I moved to D Wing.

Long-termers and lifers were a different ball game. These were adult women — most of them older than my 25 years. Here were most of the country's category A women — those needing the highest level of security.

Those who had had been convicted of murder and offences against the state, women we would now called terrorists; those serving long sentences of over six years and those transferred to the wing for internal reasons. This was not a psychotherapeutic unit although psychiatrists worked with a number of women on the wing. The officers were not expected to work in the same way as the DX staff and were more like traditional prison officers.

I settled into the life of the wing and was soon immersed in new problems and issues. This was my first real opportunity to work with women often many years older than myself. Many of them with husbands, partners and children.

One of the greatest challenges I faced there came when one of the women, Faith, a Nigerian, who was eventually sentenced to five years, stopped eating. She had been allocated to D Wing despite being 'on remand' because she was thought to be vulnerable to attack from other women; it was easier to observe her on D Wing. She was charged with importing drugs on a huge scale but more importantly had involved a small child as a 'mule'—the child carried the drugs. It wasn't a protest—she wasn't on hunger strike, she just ate less and less until, to all intents and purposes, she wasn't eating at all. She continually complained about her stomach but the medical staff were not convinced.

On D Wing the women were allowed to eat in their rooms. They would collect their meals from the landing and then take the food back to their cells to eat socially with others. Faith wasn't friendless despite her offence and her friends on the wing came to me extremely concerned. Could I do something? Obviously I talked to Faith, and spent time with her at meal times. She said that she didn't like the food and could she have things that she liked? This wasn't possible of course. I referred her to the wing doctor and the prison hospital. The doctor still wasn't sympathetic and would not admit Faith to the hospital. She said that Faith would best be helped by being with her friends on the wing. Over the weeks, Faith lost weight; I remember feeling desperate—this woman was in my care. I raised the matter at the morning knitting circle and despite the Governor being qualified as a medical doctor, I received no help, support or advice. Faith was to remain on the wing. By now her friends were anxious.

Faith kept saying she couldn't eat prison food—she had violent pains in her tummy. However she was sure that she could manage some special bread and yams. Yes, and some particular biscuits. And spices to put in her food. The list began to grow. Clutching at straws, how was I to get this food? The prison wasn't going to provide it and I knew that I mustn't pay for it and neither could her family or friends send it in.

Some prisoners attracted a lot of public attention and Faith was no exception. At this time, she had not been convicted or sentenced and was therefore, subject to different rules and regulations to those applicable to sentenced women. She frequently received letters from admirers. Rather startling considering her alleged offences but she was a controversial figure in some respects. I was able to read these letters to her and ask her what responses she wanted me to send on her behalf. One letter suggested that she back a race horse called Demon Drink. Obviously she couldn't do this but I could. One of my colleagues was a racing enthusiast and had an account at Ladbrokes; I doubt I would have done it if it hadn't been easy—but it was simple to ask my colleague to put a £1 on Demon Drink—he was to run at the Cheltenham Festival. He ran and he won. I can't remember how much I won but enough to buy Faith food.

No, she did not eat it.

Yes, the other women were jealous.

Yes, the officers thought I was favouring a particular woman.

No, I had not told the Governor or the deputy governor.

Faith continued to lose weight dramatically and eventually the prison hospital conceded and admitted her. She was then transferred to an outside hospital having been diagnosed with a rare and severe digestive tract complaint.

Thirty years ago her condition was well outside most people's experience, be they a medic or otherwise. I certainly knew nothing about this illness. I visited Faith on a number of occasions until I was transferred to Hindley Borstal, a long way from Holloway. Faith eventually recovered and returned to prison to serve her sentence.

Looking back with today's knowledge and experience of this condition, it is difficult to understand why the prison medical staff, the wing doctor or the Governor did not recognise the seriousness of this condition. But as I say this was over 30 years ago.

The wing doctor sadly committed suicide not long after these events. Perhaps she was not able to focus on much outside her own misery. The Governor too is now dead. I did not understand, I still do not understand her response to my situation.

What do I feel now?

Amazed that things like this happened.

The situation with Faith was serious in many ways. Looking back I feel I should have had help and support. But...

I was young and arrogant. I liked my superiors but I can't remember ever asking for their advice, I don't remember ever discussing my concerns with them. And neither do I remember them ever talking to me, offering any support. However, if they did—I probably didn't listen and I don't suppose I ever behaved as if I needed anyone else's counsel. I did talk to my peers and they were helpful and supportive but I suspect that I didn't really take their words seriously if they were contrary to my own thinking.

And yet I did listen to my officers.

I remember vividly a knock on the door of my office some weeks after I took up my very first posting at Holloway. In came all the staff on duty—five of them, all dressed in their blue uniforms with their chains swinging, headed up by the senior officer, Mrs Freeman.

'Madam,' she said, 'we like you very much, but if you continue to behave in this arrogant and aloof manner we will not work with you any longer. If you do not include us and if you continue to favour the trainees over us—we must part'...or something to this effect.

I learned and I learned fast. These officers became my good friends and were incredibly supportive. I learned to work with them—recognising that the wing would be successful if my management (we didn't talk about leadership then) of my staff team was effective. They gave me succour during the hard times that followed and I know that they often supported me against the opinions of fellow officers who didn't know me. There was a downside! They all smoked—this was the 1970s—and when I went out with them I succumbed to smoking the occasional menthol cigarette in a long holder. I was a fervent anti-smoker then and remain so to this day but I was prepared to move some way towards them in social situations against my own principles. I wanted to be accepted and I needed them.

By the time I was posted to Bullwood Hall as deputy governor I was 28-years-old. Another new ball game. This time I didn't have responsibility for a particular wing or house. I had a much broader remit with some specific responsibilities including my major role, deputising for the Governor in her absence. My staff team was the whole staff compliment but of course it wasn't *my* team.

I had to make a real adjustment. No longer could I work with trainees in depth myself—I had to learn to work through the officers, including the other assistant governors, guiding them and supporting them. I had been prepared for this at Hindley Borstal where it was more difficult for me, as a female AG, to work with the boys directly in the same way as I had done at Holloway. At Hindley, my principal officer worried that I might put myself at risk if I interviewed boys on my own or walked the landings without a male escort. I didn't see it this way but I compromised and learned to work through my officers. I had to convince my team that it was okay to take a greater personal interest in the boys and look for opportunities to support them. It wasn't that officers didn't want to do this—it was just that it appeared to be counter-culture for officers to display care or concern. I perceived the prevailing prison officer culture to be quite macho. I'd like to think that we did change the way officers worked with boys on East House during my time.

Being a deputy governor tested me in many ways. I was not *the* Governor and yet I was required to 'act up' in that role when she was away which amounted to a considerable length of time over the year. But I wasn't the boss. The most difficult issue I had to cope with was the differing styles of our leadership. My Governor, who came from a medical background, was some 17 years older than I. She believed in doing most things herself including dealing with recalcitrant borstal trainees physically. Bullwood was always a hothouse. Ninety adolescent females, many with severe behavioural problems confined in close quarters was never going to be a haven of peace and quiet. The 'Agro' alarm bell rang frequently (Agro was a trade name and was written on the bell).

One particular instance illustrates this difference vividly. Three trainees had barricaded themselves in their cell. The Governor, myself, and one of my male AG colleagues had been called up to the house as soon as the incident began.

Three trainees had successfully barricaded their cell door using their bunks and drawer unit. Two feisty black girls and one difficult white youngster were giving the staff a hard time shouting obscenities; nothing anyone could say was going to make a blind bit of difference and they were spoiling for fight.

The Governor sent for the all-male maintenance team who arrived with appropriate tools including a sledge hammer. The girls, sensing that force was going to be used, set fire to their bedding. The Governor, deciding that it would take too long to open the door with the jack, took the sledge hammer herself and started to knock down the brick wall from the adjacent cell. The rest of us looked on in amazement—there were at least three strong men ready and waiting. A rather rotund dumpy figure, she swung the hammer with enthusiasm. Having breached the wall, the Governor eventually gave the implement to one of the men (I suppose she had struck a blow for equality?). She then ordered the fire hoses to be deployed.

By this time the girls were hysterical and angry. The other trainees, locked in their rooms, were giving moral support—banging on the doors, screaming obscenities. The place was filled with officers and a 'good old' fight ensued. I had no choice but to join the scrap. I still have my key chain with its buckle well and truly bent by a well-aimed kick. Inevitably, the trainees were over-whelmed, subdued and carted off to the Punishment Unit.

My Thoughts on barricades
By a borstal trainee

I, myself, think barricades are quite amusing as long as you have company. I have experienced only one myself and I never enjoyed myself so much in the five months I've been here. I only lasted forty hours but it was fun while it lasted. As long as you can pay the consequences later, your laughing.

I had 14 days loss of pay and privileges. I was quite lucky really. While my two friends and I were in there we had a fresh supply of water every day. But as soon as the water stopped we were done for. We had no option but to break the barricade down ourselves and give up.

But still, not to worry, I can still laugh and that's the main thing.

Article submitted to wing magazine *In and Out*

Leadership like this made no sense to me. Of course there were times when one had to get involved physically as Governor, but surely, only as a last resort. We all knew that borstal girls normally gave up of their own accord.

I wasn't happy with my Governor's 'hands on' style of leadership. Leading from the front was one thing but spoiling for a fight and acting in ways which might be seen as inappropriate jarred.

During my time at Bullwood we had one major riot. Mrs Joanna Kelley, the assistant director of the women's service describing Bullwood in a short report in December 1974, commented 'the stormy turbulence of Bullwood continues'. Stormy and turbulent it was. A group of girls on House Three overpowered their officers, took their keys and let all the girls out on two houses to run riot round the building.

> The noise is deafening — sound ricocheting off low ceilings and echoey walls — girls scream as only girls can do. Radiators clang and thud against the floor as they are pulled off the walls by youngsters who have turned demonic for a while. Chairs are thrown, plates and pans crash. Many don't care who they hurt in their hysteria and excitement. No one knows what is round each corner.

> A note I wrote on a scrap of paper after the incident

And I didn't know. I asked two officers to go to a particular location not knowing what the dangers were. They walked straight into a group of howling banshees who attacked them. Fortunately no real physical harm was done but I doubt these two officers relished going along corridors alone for some time after this. I didn't think — so folk were hurt.

Everyday something different happened. One never knew what each day would hold. I was continually challenged by amazing situations. All of these made a significant impression upon me and have remained with me over the years. I learned so much and as my leadership career developed I used what I had learned. Now, working in management development, I talk about what I learned. The greatest lessons for me were those which taught me the responsibilities of leadership. Other people paid for my mistakes — they paid when I got things wrong.

I enjoyed working in secure establishments. Every day was different. I never knew what was coming. It was exciting in many ways. I certainly had my ups and downs and was regularly in bother with someone. My colleagues tell me that I frequently talked about leaving—I was so frustrated. I didn't suffer fools gladly and was often highly critical of 'senior management' as we would say now. Their response was different—they were tolerant of me in many ways.

My colleagues—officers and governor grades—were an amazing group of people. Many had lived through the Second World War as young adults and brought all that experience and expertise with them into the service. Others were badly damaged and scarred emotionally. There were those who had professional backgrounds—from medicine, teaching or social work. Many came from the services. Some like me were young, idealistic souls.

A number of officers had had long careers within the service of 30 years or more—they had seen huge changes; they had joined in the days when hanging was still on the statute book and Aylesbury was the only borstal for girls. When women prisoners wore prison dress and bread and water was a permitted punishment.

And there were the oddballs—'Dotty'—who liked to have her breakfast the night before because it 'saved time in the morning'. But more of this later.

Cameo 4: A glimpse of a personal cry?

At 6.35 pm on 29 January 1977 the telephone rang. Principal Officer Miss Frobisher told me there was trouble on Martyn House. I went over immediately. The Governor was on leave and I was responsible for the institution in her absence.

My typed report of the evening's events, print now fading after 30 years, reads 'I went in and went straight to Martyn House. About three officers, Miss Frobisher and Mr Frank were standing in the corridor. Mr Frank came down to the end of the wing and informed me that Kristine Bruton had Miss Taylor hostage in the office, together with Miss Right. Miss Taylor had been stabbed. Two other trainees were also in the office with Kristine'.

Through the window of the office door I could see Pauline Smith and Kristine holding a knife close to Miss Taylor.

I asked if I could come in and the door was opened for me. I went in. Kristine said 'If you come any nearer or jump me I will hurt Tatty' (the trainees' nickname for Miss Taylor).

I said I wasn't going to do anything only talk. I sat down on a chair near the office door.

Miss Taylor had blood on her jumper and it appeared that she had been stabbed.

I talked to Kristine and asked her to give up the knife. I asked her to put it on the table. She said that she couldn't. Everyone on Martyn House had let her down. She had nothing to lose now. The object of the exercise was to get out of the borstal. She was going to beat the system and win (Kristine had been convicted of using a firearm to resist arrest and had previous convictions for sending letters threatening to murder).

I resolved the situation after six hours. Just before one am, the trainees were finally removed to the Punishment Unit.

Much happened during those six hours. I had called in the psychiatrist, Dr Redman, who worked with the trainees on this unit to see if he could persuade them to give up and release their hostage. Eventually, we managed to get the girls to let Miss Taylor go by my taking her place but we could not get Kristine to give up her knife or persuade the other two girls to give up.

As the hours dragged on, Dr Redmond and I played cards and noughts and crosses with the girls, and chatted away to them. It was rather boring really but I made a conscious choice to wait until the girls were tired and really wanted the situation to end. I didn't expect them to give up — that would be to lose too much face — I knew that we would get to a point where they would put up little resistance. Then I would take action. Borstal girls with the kinds of histories these three had could be hysterical and very dangerous when cornered. There had been much posturing and waving of the sizeable kitchen knife when staff members came to the door but — as the evening wore on — this happened less frequently. The girls wanted to end the situation without losing face (Where did the knife come from? — Nicked from the cookery kitchen).

I knew what the Governor would do if I called her in. She would tackle Kristine physically. After midnight I asked Kristine to give up the knife or I would call in the Governor. She refused. I called. True to form, the Governor came straight in and assisted by Dr Redman, grabbed Kristine, who put up no resistance.

The situation was resolved without further violence but my actions incurred the wrath of my Governor and the displeasure of head office. My Governor maintained that I should have called her in. I disagreed for two reasons. Firstly, my understanding was that I was the governor in charge — she was on leave. Secondly, I believed that the Governor's approach to the situation at any time other than the opportune moment would very likely have resulted in more violence and possible serious harm to the Governor herself or other staff. The knife was a significant weapon; the trainee wielding it had already hurt one member of staff and consequently hadn't much to lose by hurting someone else. She would have been well-supported by the other two trainees. Ill-timed intervention might also have provoked the trainees to commit further serious and violent offences.

My actions had called the Governor's style into question. The staff were split in two in their opinion. I'd like to think that some thought I was right — I know others certainly thought that I was wrong. The atmosphere throughout the borstal was tense and difficult for everyone for several days.

A week or so later we had a debriefing with the Prison Service's director of operations, an assistant controller P5 Division, two Governor Is from P5, the senior woman Governor I from P4 Division and a police adviser. I remember little other than a total lack of support from anyone.

Sometime later I was called up to head office to see the Governor I who had responsibility for the female establishments. She was kind but offered no real support. I do not remember her even saying 'Well done'. Perhaps she did but it certainly left no impression with me. Of course there are pros and cons on both sides. I did make mistakes. I had my keys on me when I went into the office with Kristine and the other two trainees. Had they overpowered me they could have taken my keys — the Governor's keys. Maybe I prolonged the situation and made it worse. I should not have 'used' the Governor in the way I did. But …..no-one else got hurt and the situation was resolved without further incident. The trainees did not have even more serious charges to answer.

The three trainees stood trial and were convicted. Kristine was sent to a special hospital.

Looking back, I felt unsupported and alone. It was difficult for the assistant governors to support me for obvious reasons. My close friends were not nearby. It had been a difficult, long and stressful situation but no-one appeared to think about what I might be going through.

CHAPTER 11

Will We Have to Call You 'Madam' Now?

The staff structure in the Prison Service was modelled on the military system—commissioned officers and other ranks became governor grades and, confusingly, prison officers. The term 'warders' had been replaced in 1919 but even today it is still sometimes used by the uninitiated.

Prospective officers joined the service as prison officers under training (POUTS); having completed this they became *prison officers*. The first rung of the promotion ladder took them to *senior officer* and then *principal officer*. The most senior rank to which officers could aspire was *chief officer* unless they chose to cross the divide and apply for selection to assistant governor. Every prison and borstal had a defined number of basic grade officers, senior officers, principal officers and one chief officer. Sometimes the most senior officer in charge of a wing would be a principal officer and sometimes a senior officer. These career prison officers were all *established staff*.

There was one other category of officer—*temporary officer*. These were people who joined the service on a temporary basis as the name implies—people who had not gone through the formal officer training process and consequently were not career officers. They could not be formally promoted and were trained on the job. Bullwood Hall had a significant number of temporary officers—local married women who wanted to work in the borstal but whose family commitments didn't allow them to spend a period of time away from home training; their family commitments also meant that they were not free to be posted to other prisons. Many people recruited as assistant governors from outside the service were recommended to work as temporary officers before they went to the staff college at Wakefield; this was their first taste of prison life as I explained in *Chapter 2*.

My time as a temporary officer at Bullwood Hall was an invaluable experience for many reasons. I gained some understanding of what it was like to be a borstal officer, subject to the day-to-day pressure of continuous contact with difficult and disruptive inmates. Later, as a member of the governor grade, I could walk away but as an officer I couldn't.

My governor grade colleagues — those of us called 'Mam' (in the women's service of course) fitted into the 'commissioned officer' structure. We joined as assistant governor IIs (normally referred to as AG Two), our next promotion was to AG I, then governor III, governor II and finally Governor I. We in the women's service were more fortunate than the men in some respects. There were fewer of us and we were likely to be promoted more quickly. They had to wait for 'dead men's shoes'. I remember many a conference where colleagues would be pouring over the staff list—working out what would happen when so and so retired, left the service or died.

I was promoted to AG I three years after I was posted to HMP Holloway. My male colleagues were kind but it must have been galling for them. I was probably the first of the 1970-71 Assistant Governor Staff Course to be promoted. One of my good friends wrote me a note

21.8.74
Will I have to call you 'Madam' now?
Congratulations,
Luv
Bob

Who were we all? There were 54 of us on the 23rd Prison Service Staff Course, 51 men and three women. Three or four of our number had been prison officers and had passed the selection board for assistant governor; we came from all walks of life. Probation officers, a priest, teachers like me, Navy, RAF and Army officers. Our predecessors on earlier courses had come from similar backgrounds — an even greater number coming from the armed services — many prison officers were also ex-military.

The Second World War had ended just 25 years previously when I joined the service in 1970. Serving prison officers and governor grades had seen war service; they had been buffeted about by cataclysmic events or had grown up in a world shaped by fighting and conflict. In 1970, with a Polish father and an English mother I was born as a result of the war and its influence was very real to me as I grew up. The assistant director who recruited me was an early graduate of Girton College, Cambridge who had worked in the department of pre-history at the *Musée de l'Homme* in Paris before joining the Admiralty as a welfare officer during the war. My Governor at Hindley Borstal had been a Japanese prisoner-of-war and had suffered appalling privations. My first Governor at Holloway had been in the Women's Royal Army Corps and worked resettling Polish refugees after the war. My deputy governor at Holloway was displaced from Bohemia and came to England as a refugee. One of my assistant governor colleagues at Holloway was married to a Jewish academic who had come to Britain to escape Hitler just before the war; and another had been evacuated from London as a child during the war and joined the Women's Land Army as soon as she could. These were fascinating individuals whose outlook on life and views on imprisonment had been shaped by their own lives. Together with many others they contributed a richness to the service from which I, and younger members like me, benefited enormously.

The Prison Service and its borstal section in particular had been influenced by a number of very significant and larger than life personalities. Sir Alexander Paterson (1884-1947) who was a member of the Prison Commission probably made a more significant contribution to the development of a humane penal system than anyone else since Elizabeth Fry. He did this through his tireless enthusiasm and compassion, and the force of his personality. Dame Lillian Barker (1874-1955), the first female assistant commissioner of prisons appointed in 1935 and Charity Taylor (1914-1988), the first female Governor of Holloway Prison in 1945, appointed when she was only 31, achieved amazing changes in women's prisons through the force of their personalities, passion and conviction. Mrs Joanna Kelley, assistant director was no exception. There is no doubt that these charismatic individuals created their own fiefdoms over which they held sway. However during the 1970s this very personalised leadership in the Prison Service was becoming discredited in favour of a more modern management-oriented approach.

I was fortunate in that I worked with a very dedicated set of women. I didn't appreciate this at the time and it was only later that I realised how much I owed to these remarkable people.

Flyaway Hair

Dorothy Wing retired as Governor of Holloway Prison in 1972 and died on 23 January 1993 in Kington, Herefordshire. She appears to have had no next of kin and I look back now with real regret; she was my first Governor and she had a soft spot for me. After her retirement I went to stay with her on several occasions, but sadly I didn't maintain that contact other than at Christmas for a few years. The busyness and self-importance of youth.

Mrs Wing left the service unsung and uncelebrated in the main, other than by her friends and colleagues at Holloway and the women for whom she was responsible. I have not been able to find an obituary for her which, if true, is disgraceful—she ran the most infamous and significant women's prison in the country—HMP Holloway, for six years. She didn't receive an honour of any kind despite existing precedent for someone of her seniority and her achievement. Dorothy Wing alone 'carried the can' for the Myra Hindley walk in the park episode. I believe it is highly likely that she had consulted her superiors in the Prison Department about this disastrous event which I described in *Chapter 5* and that they chose to distance themselves from a huge error of judgement. The relevant Prison Department papers are not available to the public and will not be released for 30 years. Whose error was it?

Just before her retirement, Dorothy Wing was interviewed by prisoners for *Behind the Times*, D Wing's magazine.

Mrs Wing entered the Prison Service in 1956 after having spent nearly 20 years in the Auxiliary Territorial Service—the women's branch of the army in WWII—later known as the Women's Royal Army Corps. Her interest in prisons was aroused by her friend Miss Melanby, then Commissioner of Prisons, who arranged for her to visit East Sutton Park (a girls' borstal) and Holloway. We asked Mrs Wing her first impressions and she told us she found Holloway 'terribly grim' and by contrast, East Sutton Park 'delightful'.

Mrs Wing joined the service and after two years was transferred to Holloway. During her five years as an Assistant Governor she introduced Group Counselling.

Mrs Wing explained to us that she was not very taken by the idea of Group Counselling until attending a 12 week course at Wakefield which awakened an interest in her for the project. She told us with enthusiasm of the closeness which developed between staff and inmates due to Group Counselling. Groups were comprised of about ten women each, and an outside Visiting Psychologist came in once a week to confer with staff and help them with any problems that had developed...

...in January 1967 Mrs Wing became Governor of Holloway. When asked if she remembered her first reaction, she said 'I was terrified'. There is no doubt that Mrs Wing was instrumental in many changes which had taken place in Holloway in the past five years. The introduction of the rule that women could wear their own clothing was championed by Mrs Wing. She felt the increase in morale from this was tremendous. The modernisation of the laundry 'now torn down due to reconstruction' is remembered as one of Mrs Wing's achievements. The introduction of men as cooks, teachers and education officers in Holloway was also Mrs Wing's idea, an innovation of which she was particularly pleased since this change was welcomed as being more natural.

Filling in a few gaps, Mrs Wing married in 1931; history does not relate what happened to this marriage but she later joined the ATS. She was commissioned in 1941 and promoted to major in 1949 where she worked with the Polish forces resettling soldiers, sailors and airmen who could not return to occupied Poland. Although I was not aware of this at the time, she probably 'resettled' my father in 1946.

The walk in the park was Mrs Wing's downfall. There is no doubt that she had a good relationship with Myra Hindley—she had after all been Governor when Myra was committed to prison in 1965 and consequently had known her for many years. Mrs Wing's letter to me reproduced in *Chapter 5* mentions Myra in quite an affectionate way. I believe that both Mrs Wing and Joanna Kelley expected Myra to be released on parole in time and had been planning for this. A driving licence had been obtained for Myra in preparation for this—in a new name of course. I remember Mrs Wing showing me this although I cannot remember why she did so. It was kept in her office safe. I find it difficult to believe that she obtained it off her own bat. I also remember Myra talking to me about these plans—she expected that initially she would probably go to a convent.

Mrs Wing had overseen the upgrading of security arrangements at Holloway in response to the imprisonment of serious female offenders including Myra. Interestingly, just before the walk in the park, Myra had been downgraded—reclassified as a category B inmate from high security category A; this reduced the level of security the Prison Service was required to implement for her.

There is an account of an interview with Mrs Wing on a journalist's web site in which it is suggested that she took Myra out on a number of occasions prior to that fateful day, including a visit to the Tutankhamen Exhibition. The walk in the park appears to have become public when an officer at Holloway reported the fact that I had taken Myra out of the prison to her boyfriend in a male prison. He apparently alerted the press. Unbeknown to most, all Victorian closed prisons had a back door—this could be used to release notorious prisoners at the end of their sentence or when moving prisoners to avoid disturbances and publicity. Holloway certainly had one, far away from the main gate and it would have been possible for Mrs Wing to take Myra out of this backdoor gate but I am sceptical. As are my colleagues. We don't believe Mrs Wing took Myra out on any other occasion. If she had, why didn't she use the same route out of the prison on the walk in the park day? Had Myra been out previously I think she would have told me—she would have had no reason not to. Perhaps the truth might be known in 30 years' time. What was the assistant director of the women's service, Mrs Kelley's, role in the aftermath? And the Home Secretary of the day, Robert Carr?

As a result of the walk in the park Dorothy Wing was retired in disgrace—quietly with no public acknowledgment of her long service and contribution.

It is easy to look back and see her as a victim. In some respects she was—a victim of her loyalty and adherence to the Official Secrets Act. Working under her governorship gave a completely different view; she was a 'tough cookie' in many respects. She didn't put up with nonsense from anyone but both the women and officers liked her very much. Short and dumpy and a chain smoker, she was reserved and taciturn about her own private life but very kind and interested in the lives of her women and staff.

As my Governor, she wasn't too pleased about the shoes thrown at her when my borstal girls took to the roof in protest. But Mrs Wing didn't hold that against me—she didn't harbour grudges. A drink at lunchtime was the social norm in those days and after a particularly good lunch she could be seen putting out a hand to steady herself against the rails above the Centre as she toured the prison. If we really wanted to gauge her mood we looked at her hair. If it was *flyaway*—not a good time to ask for anything! She was a very human individual.

Kington
My dear Joanna

I hope this gets to you as the address is a bit vague.

I think you are very brave to take on your job as Head of the Special Unit for that age group but I sure you will make a success of it.

Naturally I am sorry that the Prison Service couldn't offer you the advantages to keep you but from what I hear from Audrey there have been many changes!

As you know I'd love to see you one day may be you can stop off for a night?

Love and best wishes
Dorothy Wing

Dorothy Wing was a committed and humane governor. She was a loyal and devoted public servant of the old school and did not deserve the disgrace heaped upon her at the end of her career. I remember her as a kind insightful and supportive person.

Treading the Boards

Her ambition was to be an actress; Audrey Stern was working towards this as an understudy and stage manager with the Shanklin Theatre on the Isle of Wight, about to become the front of house manager when France fell in June 1940. I asked her recently why she joined the Prison Service and she responded by saying that she always wanted to be an actor and joining the service just happened.

Audrey came from Jewish stock and met her husband, Walter Stern, at one of the clubs for Jewish refugees she was helping to run right at the beginning of the war. After they married they were bombed out of their flat in Highgate and as a result moved to St Albans. Audrey wanted to do something serious for the war effort and as there was a Red Cross Unit over the road, she joined as a Red Cross nurse.

Never one to dwell on the downside of anything Audrey wrote of her experiences in a book which records the lives of local residents in North London.

I did a few sessions of 'dental day' at the local hospital. This entailed standing on
one side of the dentist's chair holding a kidney dish. On the other side was the
dentist and in front was a nurse with what I suppose was an ether mask which
she slapped over the patient's face. Once the patient was 'out', the dentist pulled
teeth and dropped them in my kidney dish. Several women patients came in with
fetching hair-dos, and I was astonished to see that once the mask was over their
faces, their hair stood on end and danced. Nurse was quite unfazed. 'It's the lice'
she said. 'The women don't wash their hair because they don't want to lose the
waves, so of course they get infected'.

Then I was moved to Cell Barnes Hospital, which had been for the demented,
but Barts was evacuated there. I was sent at once to a ward packed with the seriously injured from the London blitz. There was a woman there who was delirious
and my job was to watch her and stop her falling out of bed, but one look at her
terribly injured face and I promptly fainted. Coming to I found sister patting my
cheek and saying 'Pull yourself together, get up and get on with what you have
been told to do.' So I did, but the experience had come as something of a shock
after only six weeks in the Red Cross learning how to bandage a sprained wrist.

As many of the trained nursing personnel were still holed up in France, I also
worked in the operating theatres, fetching and carrying sterilised instruments and
watching operations on the hands of badly burnt pilots. I really loved nursing
and applied to do my SRN, but Matron would have none of it. 'I know you girls
with husbands stationed in England, you always run off camp' following which,
of course we did. My husband thought he would be called into the RASC (Royal
Army Service Corps) as he was educated and literate, but the letter S seems to
have been dropped and instead he was called up into the Royal Armoured Corps,
which was using tanks!

…After the war ended, my husband was selected for the War Crimes Commission and was at Nuremberg for the trials. I had let out the sitting room and
the main bedroom, retaining just the small bedroom, and often friends would
come and sleep on the floor. It wasn't difficult getting things for babies during

the war, we would be allowed eggs, orange juice and cod liver oil. It was the old people who suffered, babies have never been healthier.

Audrey eventually joined the Prison Service as an assistant governor. When I met her, she was in charge of the Mother and Baby Unit. Audrey only served at Holloway — a special arrangement with Mrs Kelley. This caused some irritation with one or two other assistant governors who saw it as favouritism — some of them didn't want to be posted to borstals way out in the sticks, far from London. Audrey's very normal life, married with a family gave her a perspective that sometimes eluded the rest of us single career women whatever age we were. Her common sense and calmness came to my aid on many an occasion. I remember vividly railing against the restrictions of the service and the prison one morning, saying how lucky those who had been involved in the war had been — they had something to fight for — how it had been a great time for some. Audrey reproved me sadly and gently. I was of course ashamed of my outburst and came to like and respect her enormously for her humour, wisdom and fairness. I also got to know Audrey's husband Walter; he was a delightful man who taught Economic History at the London School of Economics. I was much in awe of him because he was a serious academic and I knew nothing about economics. Had I known that Mick Jagger was one of his students, I might have been less intimidated!

Audrey looked after Myra Hindley at Holloway for many years and remained in touch with her, visiting her regularly over the whole of her sentence until Myra died in 2002, long after she herself had retired. Audrey was never 'taken in' by Myra and I always found a conversation with her about Myra invaluable; I also visited Myra for a number of years before she died and Audrey would give me an objective no nonsense view of Myra's sometimes manipulative activities and relationships which ensured I maintained a balanced view.

A visit to Audrey is always a joy. When I ask her to look back on her days in the service she still says she would have preferred to tread the boards. I am sure she would have been a great actress but I would have missed a good friend and wise counsellor.

A Woman of Convictions and Conscience

I'd like to think that I would not have joined the Prison Service if hanging had still been on the statute book. I was perturbed that a miscarriage of justice could result in the execution of an innocent person. It would also have meant that, as a governor in the service, I would have had to accompany a prisoner to the scaffold. But it was different for one of my colleagues—she did consider this issue. Writing to me recently:

> I was far too young to join the service and there was another difficulty in that I
> also had a strong conviction against capital punishment then in force.

Muriel Allen joined the service in 1966, retiring in 1990 after 24 years. She didn't come from the relatively more affluent background that many of her colleagues had enjoyed.

> I was born in May 1931 in South London, in a working class family. At that time
> I was the third daughter. Eventually there were seven daughters and three sons.
> In the 1930s there was an epidemic of childhood diphtheria and scarlet fever.
> Infant mortality was very high. I caught diphtheria and almost died. I was sent
> to a children's hospital in Surrey for convalescence. Altogether I was away from
> home for over a year. The second major disruption of my life was the outbreak
> of war in 1939 and the mass evacuation of children of school age from London
> to the country, in the care of our teachers to an unknown destination. Three of
> us sisters went; the sister in charge of the party was ten years old. I was eight
> and the other six. Under school age children were left at home with our parents.
>
> We were taken with seven other children from our school together with our
> teacher to live in the home of a millionaire on the outskirts of Sevenoaks in
> Kent. This was possible because many of his staff had joined the forces so we
> had their accommodation. Our host called his family nanny out of retirement to
> look after us. Education was basic at the local country church school which was
> overwhelmed with the influx from London.
>
> We were treated extremely well and given new clothes for winter. There was a
> great contrast with conditions at home. Most of the war years were spent there;

spitfires fought the battle of Britain overhead from nearby Biggin Hill aerodrome, the nearness of the Kent coast and the fall of France made us aware of other dangers. The rest of the family were dispersed, some to Norfolk, some with our parents to Cornwall while we remained in Kent. Our house in South London was bombed in 1943. After D day and towards the end of the war, father found a five bed roomed house in a leafy suburb in Surrey and brought us gradually back together to become a united family once more. By the end of the war, I was fourteen years old, then the school leaving age. In the summer of 1945 when the war was over I left school for the world of work. Due to my poor education and general disruption I had no chance of an attempt at matriculation and there was a pressing need to contribute to the family budget. I began my first job as a junior clerk at the local Town Hall three days after my fourteenth birthday.

The war had left me with serious outlook on life and a profound thankfulness that my entire family had survived it without loss or damage apart from the bombing of our first home in London.

The post war years and my late teens gave me a growing awareness that I had a vocation and that was to be of service to others in some way. The focus of this became the Prison Service. A number of notorious cases, miscarriages of justice and unease at the difficulties faced by disadvantaged defendants versus the brilliance of Crown prosecutors no doubt influenced my increasing social conscience. My first office job was followed by a variety of clerical work jobs, usually prompted by small steps in promotions and pay. An older friend of mine joined the Women's Land Army and spoke of her adventures and fun. I put my age up and joined her. After four carefree years in the company of other young women doing hard physical work in dairy farming, I left with another friend to travel in Europe and had great adventures in Finland, Denmark and France. After three years of travelling I came home to England to settle down to a career in the residential child care service and inevitably found myself working with young delinquents in Remand Homes and Approved Schools. I was able to take the opportunities this offered to gain qualifications at this time.

I read everything I could find about the Criminal Justice System although I did not always understand what I was reading as I had no guidance. I waited patiently for the abolition of capital punishment, working in support of organisations such as the Howard League for Penal Reform. By the time Sydney Silverman's Private Member's Bill was finally accepted, receiving the Royal Assent in November 1965 and becoming law, I had been promoted to Deputy Superintendent of a juvenile remand home for girls in Croydon. I felt able to respond to an advertisement for Assistant Governors in the Prison service which clearly stated 'Educationally, graduate level desirable but not essential.

Muriel Allen probably had the toughest of times within the women's service. As she says in her letter, she was to a large extent self-educated — extremely well-read and knowledgeable about the criminal justice system and politics. She hadn't been to the right school and didn't come from the right kind of family. Nor had some others but somehow this was glossed over for them but not for Muriel. There was no two ways about it, Joanna Kelley, the assistant director didn't like Muriel and she made this obvious. As noted earlier, the women's service was Mrs Kelley's fiefdom — she held personal power over all of us. I was fortunate — my face fitted — after all we shared a name. Despite my youth and lack of experience I was promoted ahead of Muriel which was unwarranted, unfair and cruel. Mrs Kelley appeared to ensure that Muriel had a really hard time. This was the downside of the cult of the person-ality — personal power used badly is damaging. Fortunately the governors of the female establishments were able to ameliorate some of the hurt. After Mrs Kelley's retirement in 1974, life looked up for Muriel. She gained her promotion quickly and in 1982 was promoted to be Governor of Kingston Prison in Portsmouth, then a prison for life-sentenced men. She wrote

> This appointment was also the validation of the vocation I felt from the begin-
> ning because this prison is the only penal institution in England which has an
> entire population of life sentenced men. I waited to join the prison service until
> capital punishment was abolished and now I was asked, years later, to deal with
> the consequences of abolition. Without a doubt every man in that establishment
> would have hanged under the former legislation.

Muriel achieved her BA, was chosen to receive the Royal Maundy Money at Portsmouth Cathedral, has lunched with Her Majesty Queen Elizabeth

II and was honoured with an MBE in 2012.

I owe Muriel a great debt. An invaluable source of advice for me when I arrived at Holloway, she continued to guide me though many situations throughout my Prison Service career.

Loaves of Bread and an Accordion

Hildegard Leissner always had bread in her cupboard. Lots of it. She was never far from staple food. Never again would she go hungry. Never, ever again.

Trying to piece together Hildegard's remarkable story has been difficult. My colleagues and I think she was born in Upper Bohemia in 1922. Following the Munich Agreement in 1938, the Nazis invaded her homeland which then became the Protectorate of Bohemia and Moravia; this to all intents and purposes was then subsumed into Czechoslovakia and occupied by the Nazis. During the war years the Nazis treated the population appallingly. We can remember Hildegard telling stories of how she earned money and kept herself relatively safe playing the piano accordion in bars in return for bread. Turmoil and disaster continued when Czechoslovakia was subsequently occupied by the Russian Liberation Army; the Czech authorities took reprisals against anyone they considered German and Hildegard found herself a displaced person and sent to an internment labour camp probably run by the allies. We don't know exactly how Hildegard found herself in England but we think that young inmates of the labour camp were offered freedom in England working in the Lancashire cotton mills — post-war the UK was short of labour. In return for work they received wages, accommodation and an allowance of coal. Hildegard and most of the women jumped at the chance even though most of them spoke no English — Hildegard was no exception.

She lived in a shared house with other women. The work in the cotton mills was hot and dirty and there were no filters in the mills so the air was full of fibres. It was a difficult situation and the women's lack of English was a handicap. But as Hildegard said, they were free and had money to spend, a contrast to their experiences in the camp in Bavaria when they were unpaid and just worked for food. Hildegard never forgot the English working-class woman supervisor who got a blackboard and chalk and began to teach the women English during the meal break. Later, Hildegard was befriended by a 'well to do' lady and she went to live with her as a secretary companion in Halifax. Here she found support and encouragement to continue her education. Evening classes in English helped a lot and a tutor told her about student grants for university which would be available to her once her application for naturalisation had been approved. Hildegard became a British citizen in July 1960 and applied successfully for university, taking a degree in Social Studies. It was during this course that she was sent on placement to East Sutton Park, the open borstal for girls; she enjoyed this experience and later applied to the Prison Service to become an assistant governor.

Hildegard died in 2010, after a long fight with Alzheimer's. At her funeral, Monica Carden, one of our governor colleagues said of her:

> Her early life experiences had taught her not to take life for granted. She had had a very loving family childhood but this was shattered by the conflicts in Europe ... she would say little of those troubled time but, throughout her life, she never lost the spirit of her homeland however proud she became of her adopted country—Great Britain.

My abiding memory of Hildegard was seeing her standing at the top of the wide staircase at Holloway most mornings, apparently waiting to see if her assistant governors arrived on time. This wasn't a problem for me as I lived in a tiny flat just outside the gates. However, it was more so for one of my colleagues who lived 'out' and came on the bus. She was often in bother! Hildegard didn't have to *say* anything. One just knew when she was displeased—I don't remember her having to use any words to convey her feelings. She was a formidable deputy governor but underneath it all everyone knew that she had their best interests at heart.

Many of the women and girls loved her. I have a number of cards written to her when she left prisons to take up a new post. The formal messages are often unpolished and appear sentimental but I am sure that the words reflect what the women wanted to say; the individual messages are very sincere.

> This is just a card to say
> We wish that you weren't going away

You've helped us in so many things
Your like an angel without wings
Always ready for a joke or laugh
We think you are the best of all the staff.
We hope you'll be back soon
Even if its only to do our Board Room.
What will we do if we are sick?
So hurry up and come back quick
Who is going to take hobbies for us now
But we suppose we'll have to get along somehow
On us you've made your mark
So please don't forget us at the Park
Good luck and God bless always.

Thank you so much for everything — I won't let you down and will often think about you with admiration and respect. With affection, Sally Black

Thank you for looking after me. Sonja

Well Governor, I have been to four prisons but you are the only one I have known that really cares. Freddie

Hildegard Leissner was hospitable and frequently invited the assistant governors for supper when she would give us a good stew followed by cheese; her flat was in one of the two houses flanking the gates of Holloway. There was always huge quantities of bread. The war years left deep scars which I didn't really recognise at the time. Never again would she go without bread. I learned later from my colleagues that Hildegard had often been starving during the war years and immediately afterwards; but, as I noted earlier, earned small amounts of food playing her accordion. These memories didn't cloud her enjoyment of her music and, if pressed, she would get out her accordion and play Bavarian songs and dances with great gusto. Looking back, her experiences of hardship and suffering appeared to give her an affinity with the women in her care which many of them recognised and appreciated.

Their Legacy

This richness of experience vested in my colleagues broadened my understanding of the world. These were my mentors and my friends, for they were my friends despite their being much older and often much more senior. They challenged my thinking. I didn't always like what they had to say and I no doubt went my own way most of the time. I liked and respected them as individuals—I was amazed at their fortitude and resilience. They didn't give up. Their stories played out like films to me and here they were larger than life. What they didn't know about challenge and temptation, self-discipline and what mattered in life wasn't worth knowing. Yes—I often saw things differently—I was of a different generation; sometimes their 'conservatism' irritated me. Sometimes I was 'right' if there was a 'right'. More often than not it was *different* rather than right.

They were wise, patient and tolerant women who gave so much to the inmates in their care and the staff they managed. We were the richer for knowing and working with them.

The Prison Service did have to change, of that there was no doubt but how was the invaluable experience and influence of women like these to be retained?

Women didn't just write to me. They wrote to many of my colleagues. I just happened to keep all the letters—they were important to me and I kept them because I am an inveterate hoarder.

I know little of the Prison Service now in the 21st-century although in my new role as Chair of the Friends of Guys Marsh I am learning more every day. I do know that since the 1970s 'management' has come in with a vengeance—not just to the Prison Service but to all walks of life.

Fortunately 'leadership' is now recognised and valued in a way that was not apparent in the 1970s and 1980s. I would like to think that we can look back on these amazing women, those who went before them and the many more who are unrecognised and unsung, and credit them with effective leadership in their time. We are not the better for the denigration and discrediting of individual influence. Yes—this has the potential to be pernicious but personality and charisma are an important part of effective leadership. Charisma is demonstrated in many different ways—the positive and caring aspects of the Prison Service have their roots in the achievements of charismatic individuals over many years.

CHAPTER 12

Reflections

Looking Back

Over 35 years have passed since I resigned as a member of Her Majesty's Prison Service. In many ways I regret leaving, but I know I made the right decision. If I hadn't left I would not have enjoyed the range of fabulous experiences that have been my life since then. It was the right decision for me (apart from the pension of course!) I did try to return a year or so after leaving but the service was not prepared to have me back at my old grade and being young and arrogant I didn't want to start again at the bottom of the pile. Those seven years made more impact on me than any seven since. I have tried to identify why this is and what I gained. I learned so much.

It was an *experience*. It is difficult for others who didn't share this experience to understand how it was, how it felt, albeit that my colleagues of the time and I saw, and still see, many things very differently. Rare experiences exclude others; unintentionally—but they do. Members of the armed services, policemen, firemen and medics will say the same thing. I belong to a group of women who shared something special. We shared horrors and physical fears, drama and theatre, pathos and tragedy. We got to know the pariahs of our society and met the other side of their personalities. We had the opportunity to make a difference to damaged lives.

It is difficult to understand events, feelings and happenings way outside our own lives. The majority of people have never been inside a prison—have never met someone who has been convicted of any crime, let alone a very serious offence, or served a prison sentence. But it is salutary to remember that one of our own family members, one of our friends, someone we met a at lunch party, a man we work with, a woman we greet over the fence, a youngster we have watched grow up may tomorrow be incarcerated in one of Her Majesty's establishments. Our regard for them should surely not change? We all make mistakes and make the wrong choices. People in prison are not from a different planet. They are you and I.

I feel privileged to have had such an experience. To have some under-standing of how it is for others, often some of the most vulnerable in our society. I learned how important it is to separate behaviour from the person. I learned that I could abhor a particular behaviour, find actions intolerable, find a particular crime appalling but I could still like and even respect the perpetrator.

I learned to listen; to keep my mouth shut and allow a hesitant voice to speak. To keep my mouth shut and allow myself to be roundly abused and berated. And then when calm prevailed to listen to fears and sometimes hopes.

I feel privileged to have shared others' misery and distress. Even though they knew I could walk away, they allowed me to be there with them. I, in turn, could share my optimism and energy with them. They, in their turn, often did the same for me. Relationships, despite uneven and diffi-cult circumstances can be two way. I learned how important it is to allow people to give even when they appear to be in no position to give—when they appear to have nothing to give. Giving is such an important part of self-worth and self-respect. A kind word, a card, a scrawled letter of thanks on a scrappy piece of paper, a handmade present, something bought from meagre wages—anything offered freely and accepted with grace contributes to a feeling of self-worth on both sides.

I learned that just being there for someone at that moment in time can be enough.

I know that we can call up an inner-strength in the face of physical danger. I could face down a broken bottle, I could challenge unacceptable behav-iour; I might be afraid but the other person may be far more afraid than I. I do not have to retaliate however much I want to.

I am as likely as the next person to moan about bad behaviour I see on the TV, to be a grumpy old woman—'youngsters these days......', and be horrified at reported crime. I abhor what I read in the newspapers—crimes against children, the crimes that children commit. But I know that faced with a perpetrator I will have a greater understanding of why they might have acted as they did. Nothing is black and white when it comes to human behaviour. I don't believe in 'an eye for eye and tooth for a tooth'. What led up to this person doing this? Where are they coming from?

I was not a soft touch. I learned that good and positive relationships do not depend on being soft, on giving in, being open to manipulation. They depend on respect and care for one another. Fairness and impartiality is more important than anything. Being described as 'fair' was one of the greatest accolades I received from the women.

One of the most important lessons of those seven years was a leadership lesson. I learned that if I made a mistake in my leadership others would suffer — often experiencing greater repercussions than I. As a leader, my judgement is key. Making good and informed judgements is what leadership is about and I have to take responsibility for the results of my judgement and actions.

One of the greatest challenges lay in understanding that the greater good often meant that individuals might lose out or suffer. As I became more senior I still saw myself as 'being there' for individuals but I had to balance this against the greater good of the institution. The challenge lay in finding ways to achieve both.

Through their letters I have listened again to the voices of some of the women who were such a large part of my life in the 1970s — women on both sides of the locked doors — inmates and staff. I can't imagine that the authors of these letters would have had any idea that their everyday thoughts expressed all those years ago would survive the decades.

It appears from what I read and what I hear, and from my experience at Guys Marsh, that things have changed substantially in the Prison Service since the 1970s. Physical conditions have changed for the better. Restrictions have been lifted on letter-writing and telephone calls for example. Society has changed dramatically and appears less tolerant of those who have broken the law in many ways. Security is paramount. Who runs our prisons and the way that prisons are managed has changed. Drugs and terrorism have made a substantial and very negative impact on penal establishments. The job my Prison Service colleagues do now is infinitely more demanding in some respects than in my time. Valuable and caring work continues to be done by dedicated staff. But it is not enough. The vast majority of those in prison find the system wanting in terms of helping them lead 'good and useful lives' in the future. On their release inadequately funded resettlement initiatives result in prisoners returning to environments that fail them. The cost to the public purse of not getting it right inside our prisons, of re-offending and further imprisonment is astronomical.

Many prison staff do care but sadly, so often, this care is overshadowed by reports of callous behaviour. In February 2013, the Prisons and Probation Ombudsman reported 50 investigations over the last five years where inappropriate restraint had been used. A man dying of cancer, going nowhere, handcuffed to an officer in his hospital bed. Another chained to his bed when in coma. I cannot believe that prison staff behaved in this way willingly. Sometimes government edict and poor leadership puts staff in impossible situations. Whether in the front line or in government—whoever runs our prisons, be they private or public organisations, whichever political party is in power and whatever they feel they have to promise the electorate—Winston Churchill's words must never be forgotten.

> The civilisation of a society can be judged by the way it treats its prisoners.
>
> Winston Churchill, Home Secretary 1910

Cries for help are still to be heard echoing down the landings.

Cameo 5: A glimpse of an innocent woman

Carol was 'pink'; plump and rather 'greasy'. I picture her now standing in front of me — sometimes sitting in her cell. I didn't find it easy to talk to Carol but we must have got on just fine. She made me a bookmark — she stitched 'Apart in body but not in mind' across the front of it in yellow thread. Gold tassels hang down.

Together with her husband, Carol had been found guilty of the rape and murder of a ten-year-old schoolgirl in 1970. She protested her innocence throughout her sentence — I didn't believe her — this couldn't possibly be true. Our legal system was fair. My role was to help her cope with her sentence. But Carol had faith. If nothing else, she hoped she would get parole after serving the 20 years minimum time decreed by the trial judge.

I didn't keep up with her and I have only one short note from her.

On 2nd May 1997 Carol died, 27 years after she had been convicted. According to fellow inmates she drowned herself in a pond at Cookham Wood Prison. Michael Howard, in one of his last judgements as Home Secretary, had made it clear on April 28th of that year — 'for some prisoners, a life sentence would be exactly what it was — for life.' Carol would never get parole despite having served more than 27 years.

Carol was probably the victim of miscarriage of justice and serious misconduct within the legal profession and judiciary. I say 'probably' because, despite an appeal citing new evidence including an impassioned statement from her husband that she was not involved, her appeal failed. After her death, her case was not re-opened despite the evidence apparently being compelling.

There was nothing left for her. No hope. There was no one batting for her.

We are 'apart in body but not in mind'. I didn't believe her and even though I couldn't have done much to help her — I didn't even give her the benefit of the doubt.

Personal Timeline for Joanna Kozubska, 1970-1977

Date	Age	Institution	Role	Level of responsibility	Notes
Aug–Sept 1970	24	HM Borstal, Bullwood Hall	Temporary officer	Borstal officer duties. Responsible for carrying out the duties allocated to me by my superiors.	Girls abscond from farm party, fete
28 Sept 1970	24	Staff College, Wakefield	Assistant governor under training	When on attachment to an institution I was treated as an assistant governor but had minimal authority. Visiting establishments I observed only.	Attachment to Ford open prison. Visits to: Risley Remand Centre, Askham Grange open prison, Moor Court open prison
14 June 1971	25	HMP Holloway	AG II. Assistant governor i/c FDX Wing—Borstal Recall	Responsible for the overall running of the wing, care of the inmates and leadership of staff.	Psychotherapeutic Unit run on the basis of group therapy. Girls get on to the roof of Holloway to protest against my transfer to D Wing

Date	Age	Institution	Role	Level of responsibility	Notes
			AGII. Assistant governor i/c D Wing Long-termers and lifers	Responsible for the overall running of the wing, care of the inmates and leadership of staff.	All category A—women posing greatest risk and the most notorious women—in the prison system. Other long-termers and lifers. Myra Hindley—that walk in the park
1 June 1973	27	HMB Hindley, Wigan	AG2. Assistant governor East House	Responsible for the overall running of the wing, care of inmates and leadership of staff.	Boy's borstal. house of 80 boys.
Aug 1974					Promotion to assistant governor I
10 Sept 1974	28	HM Borstal Bullwood Hall	AG1. Deputy governor	Deputising for the Governor—running the institution in her absence. Management and leadership. Responsible for specific areas such as staff training.	Only closed borstal for girls in England and Wales. Riot. Hostage situation resolved.
1977	31				I resigned from the Prison Service

Index

vulnerability *28, 69, 190*

  vulnerable prisoners *162*

W

Wakefield Staff College *xxi, 25, 28, 157*

wall-hangings *90*

Warwick Castle *33*

weaknesses *45*

weapons *170*

welfare *74, 123, 146, 152*

  welfare officer *70, 124, 175*

Wilde, Oscar *33*

wildlife *104*

Wing, Dorothy *39, 73, 76, 176*

work *86*

  assembly work *87*

  working-out *113, 116*

  workrooms *36*

writing *59, 69, 119, 134, 188*

Invisible Women:
What's Wrong With Women's Prisons
by Angela Devlin

Invisible Women is a comprehensive and graphic account of the state of women's prisons in England and Wales in the 1990s. It enables readers—especially people who have never set foot inside a prison—to 'see' the invisible women behind the bars. Since the book's publication in 1998 it has become something of a classic and is required or recommended reading on many college and practitioner courses.

'What a marvellous book…
Excellent': *Justice of the Peace*

Paperback and ebook
ISBN 978-1-872870-59-5 | 1998 | 300 pages

www.WatersidePress.co.uk

Holloway Prison:
An Inside Story
by Hilary Beauchamp
With a Foreword by Maggi Hambling

A compelling, true life account of her time working in this famous north-London prison. Hilary Beauchamp 'lifts the lid' on life inside, making the book a must for students of women's imprisonment or prison education. A unique and telling insight into life in a claustrophobic and sometimes violent atmosphere. An ideal primer on women's issues within the penal system. With 8 colour pages of original artwork.

'Rich and detailed reading in the under-researched and… under-published, area of female offending and prisonisation': *Punishment and Society*

Paperback and ebook
ISBN 978-1-904380-56-6 | 2010 | 288 pages

A Good Man Inside: Diary of a White Collar Prisoner
by Will Phillips

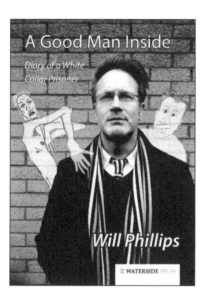

The diary of singer-songwriter Will Phillips' experiences of his time in prison written over 300 days as he reels from and makes sense of being under lock and key. A white collar criminal he sees himself as someone who should not really be in prison — as 'a good man' for whom his incarceration is doubly punitive, not practically necessary or achieving much other than the degradation and power-lessness of being in prison. But as time passes he accepts his fate and settles down to the regime, helping others and using the experience to best advantage.

- A rare white collar account of prison.
- Contains insights for anyone interested in prisoners and imprisonment.
- Set out as a diary and very easy to read.
- Illustrated by the author.
- Humorous, sometimes dark, critical, insightful and of particular interest to prison reformers

Paperback and ebook | ISBN 978-1-909976-03-0 | March 2014 | 120 pages

www.WatersidePress.co.uk

Her Majesty's Philosophers
by Alan Smith

Building on his *Guardian* pieces about teaching philosophy in prison, this is Alan Smith's account *in extenso*. Informative, entertaining, against the grain, *Her Majesty's Philosophers* highlights the artificiality of prison life. Set to be a penal affairs classic which every student of crime and punishment should read.

'Smith recounts the mundane, the bizarre and the surreal that permeates prison life, astutely observed by a remarkable story-teller': *Probation Journal*

'Both hilarious and devastating… a fascinating picture… we were delighted': *Prisoners Education Trust Newsletter*.

'Witty, insightful and above all honest… An essential read for anyone working in the criminal justice system': Clive Hopwood, Director, Writers in Prison.

Paperback and ebook | ISBN 978-1-904380-95-5 | 2013 | 216 pages

www.WatersidePress.co.uk